STRATEGIZE

Product Strategy and Product Roadmap Practices for the Digital Age

ROMAN PICHLER

Strategize: Product Strategy and Product Roadmap Practices for the Digital Age

Roman Pichler

Published by Pichler Consulting.

Editors: Rebecca Traeger; Victoria, Bill, and Carma from CreateSpace

Design: Ole H. Størksen, Roman Pichler, and Melissa Pichler

Cover photo by Ollyy/Shutterstock

ISBN Print: 978-0-9934992-1-0
ISBN ePUB: 978-0-9934992-2-7
ISBN MOBI: 978-0-9934992-0-3

To my children, Leo, Yasmin, and Kai

TABLE OF CONTENTS

ACKNOWLEDGMENTS

This book would not have been possible without the help and support of many people. I would like to thank the attendees of my product strategy and roadmap workshops, as well as my blog readers, for their feedback, comments, and questions. I would also like to thank the following individuals for reviewing this book: Jock Busuttil, Mike Cohn, Kerry Golding, Steve Johnson, Ben Maynard, Rich Mirnov, Stefan Roock, Jim Siddle, and Caroline Woodhams. Special thanks to Marc Abraham for reviewing and re-reviewing the manuscript as I changed and rewrote sections. Thank you, Geoff Watts, for helping me come to grips with self-publication; and thank you, Ole Størksen, for designing the book cover and turning my sketchy images into proper graphics. I am particularly grateful to my wife, Melissa Pichler, for all her help and support—from reviewing the manuscript and helping me with the graphics to listening to my ideas.

PREFACE

A journey of a thousand miles begins with a single step.
Lao Tzu

Developing a successful product is not down to luck, a stroke of genius, or just trying hard enough. While these factors are undoubtedly helpful, product success starts with making the right strategic decisions. The challenge for product managers, product owners, and other product people is that we are often so preoccupied with the tactics—be it dealing with an urgent sales request or writing new user stories to keep the development team busy—that we sometimes no longer see the wood for the trees. In the worst case, we take our product down the wrong path and end up in the wrong forest; we've perfectly executed the wrong strategy and are left with a product that underperforms or even bombs. This book will help you play a proactive game, make the right strategic decisions, and use them to guide the tactical work. It explains how to create a winning product strategy and an actionable product roadmap using a wide range of proven techniques and tools.

The Big Picture: Vision, Strategy, Roadmap, and Backlog

When you look up the meaning of the term *strategy*, you will probably find it defined as a plan of action to achieve a long-term goal. While this definition makes sense, developing a successful strategy for a product involves two steps: finding the right overall strategy and deciding how best to implement it. To help you focus on each step and deal with its specific challenges, I discuss them separately in this book and distinguish between a *product strategy* and a *product roadmap*. The product strategy describes how the long-term goal is attained; it includes the product's value proposition, market, key features, and business goals. The product roadmap shows how the product strategy is put into action by stating specific releases with dates, goals, and features. Figure 1 illustrates how the product strategy and roadmap relate, along with their connection to the vision and the product backlog.

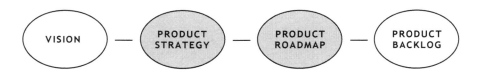

FIGURE 1: Product Strategy and Roadmap in Context

In Figure 1, the *vision* describes the ultimate reason for creating the product, the *product strategy* states how the vision will be realized, and the *product roadmap* states how the strategy will be implemented. The *product backlog* contains the details necessary to develop the product as outlined in the roadmap, such as epics, user stories, and other requirements. Note that the relationships between the elements in Figure 1 work in both directions: the product backlog can cause changes to the roadmap, for instance, which in turn may affect the strategy. For example, if the feedback from the customers and users indicates that the product does not adequately address their needs, or if the development progress is slow, then this may lead to product roadmap changes. Similarly, larger roadmap changes can cause product strategy adjustments. And if you cannot find a valid product strategy—a strategy that helps you realize the vision—then you may have to change the vision or look for a new one.

A Brief Guide to This Book

This book contains two parts. Part 1 covers product strategy practices, including determining a compelling value proposition, addressing the right segment, and selecting the right key performance indicators (KPIs). Part 2 discusses product roadmapping practices such as choosing the right roadmap format, using the right planning horizon, and reviewing the roadmap. Each practice is described in a section, and related sections are grouped into chapters. I have done my best to write the sections so that they can be read independently rather than requiring you to read the book from the beginning to the end. I have also tried to keep the sections as concise as possible, so you can read and digest them easily.

Most of the examples in this book are taken from the consumer space. The reason for this is simple: I have tried to use products that I hope you, the reader, have heard of. But the majority of practices also apply to business-to-business products. While virtually all examples are either digital products or products where software plays a key part, you can apply many of the practices to other products (although you may have to adjust them and ignore the software-specific advice).

I have written this book specifically for product executives, product managers, product owners, entrepreneurs, marketers, and others who create and manage products. You will notice, however, that I use the term *product manager* in the diagrams. My intention is not to exclude anyone who isn't called a product manager. Instead, I employ the term in a generic sense to refer to the person in charge of the product, no matter what the individual's actual job title is. While I am aware that product managers aren't always in charge of the product strategy, I believe that anyone who looks after a product and is accountable for its success should drive the creation of both the strategy and the roadmap.

PART 1: PRODUCT STRATEGY

Doing the right thing is more important than doing the thing right.
Peter Drucker

The first part of this book discusses concepts, techniques, and tools that will help you develop a winning product strategy. The practices are grouped into three chapters: strategy foundations, development, and validation. The foundation practices are key to achieving product success, no matter where your product is in its life cycle. The development practices help you create a new product and ensure the continued success of an existing one. They include techniques such as segmenting the market, working with personas, and bundling and unbundling the product, all of which are described in the pages ahead. The validation practices help you test strategy assumptions; they minimize the risk of choosing the wrong product strategy and help you create a strategy that is likely to be successful. While these practices are especially important for new products, they will also benefit an existing product whose strategy needs to change—for instance, to achieve product-market fit (PMF) or to revitalize the product to extend its life cycle.

STRATEGY FOUNDATIONS

As its name suggests, this chapter lays the foundations for the remainder of the product strategy part. It contains essential strategy concepts, techniques, and tools that will help readers who are new to the topic get up to speed; for seasoned strategy practitioners, they provide the opportunity to brush up their knowledge or close any gaps. Let's start by discussing what exactly a product strategy is.

Understand What a Product Strategy Is

What do searching on Google and booking a car on Uber have in common? Both are common technology experiences that require well-designed products that can handle varying loads, process complex interactions, and manage huge amounts of data. To achieve this, user stories have to be written, design sketches have to be created, and architecture and technology decisions have to be made. While attention to the details is necessary to create a successful product, it is easy to get lost in them. This is where the product strategy comes in: it helps you manage your product proactively by looking at the big picture.

A product strategy is a high-level plan that helps you realize your vision or overarching goal. It explains who the product is for, and why people would want to buy and use it; what the product is, and what makes it stands out; and what the business goals are, and why it is worthwhile for your company to invest in it. Figure 2 illustrates the elements of the product strategy.

FIGURE 2: The Elements of the Product Strategy

Let's take a look at the three aspects captured in Figure 2: the market and the needs, the key features and differentiators, and the business goals.

The *market* describes the target customers and users of your product: the people who are likely to buy and use it. The *needs* comprise the main problem your product solves or the primary benefit it provides. Think of a product like Google Search or Bing, which solves the problem of finding information on the Internet, compared with a product like Facebook, which provides the benefit of staying in touch with family and friends.

The *key features* and differentiators are those aspects of your product that are crucial to creating value for the customers and users and that entice people to choose it over competing offerings. Take, for example, the first iPhone and its key features of mobile Internet, an iPod-like digital-music player, and a touch screen; or the Google Chrome browser with its focus on speed, safety, and simplicity. As these two examples show, the point is not to list all product features in your strategy—that's done in the product backlog—but to focus on the three to five features that influence a person's decision to buy and use the product.[1]

---

1   As these examples show, I view features as product capabilities. Features are broken into epics in the product backlog. You can also think of a feature as a group of epics or a theme.

The *business goals* capture how your product is going to benefit your company, and why it is worthwhile for the company to invest in the product. Is it going to generate revenue, help sell another product or service, reduce costs, or increase brand equity? Being clear on the business goals allows you to select the right key performance indicators (KPIs) to measure your product's performance. Take the iPhone and the Google Chrome browser mentioned earlier. While the iPhone generates the largest portion of Apple's revenue at the time of writing, the Chrome browser does not earn any money for Google. But it does allow the company to control the way people access the Internet, and it has reduced Google's dependency on third-party browsers such as Mozilla's Firefox and Microsoft's Internet Explorer.

Note that a product strategy is not a fixed plan or something you only create for a new product: it changes as your product grows and matures. As a consequence, you should review and adjust your product strategy on a regular basis—at least once a quarter as a rule of thumb.

Think Big and Describe Your Vision

Because the product strategy is a high-level plan that describes how you intend to realize your vision or overarching goal, it is helpful to begin by capturing that vision. The vision is the ultimate reason for creating your product; it describes the positive change the product should bring about.

Why the Vision Matters

Having a vision is important, as creating and managing a successful product requires a lot of time and energy. In order to be fully committed, you have to be convinced that what you are doing is right: life is too short to work on products you don't believe in. On the positive side, if you are enthusiastic about your product, then this will help you do a great job and inspire others. Say I want to create an app that helps people become aware of what, when, and how much they eat. My vision, then, could be to help people live more healthily; the strategy would be to create an app that monitors their food intake in conjunction with a smart watch, fitness band, or smart food scales. Figure 3 illustrates this relationship.

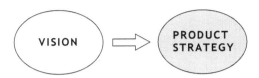

FIGURE 3: Vision and Product Strategy

Qualities of an Effective Vision

An effective vision has four qualities: it is big, shared, inspiring, and concise. A *big vision*, such as "help people eat healthily," increases the chances that people will buy into it compared to a narrow one, like "lose weight." What's more, it makes it easier to change the strategy (if necessary) while keeping the vision stable. Say that it turns out that my idea of developing a health app is ill conceived. With a big vision in place, I can explore alternatives, such as writing a book on healthy eating or offering mindfulness classes that teach people to become aware of their eating habits.

The beauty of a *shared vision* is that it motivates and unites people: it acts as the product's true north, facilitates collaboration, and provides continuity in an ever-changing world.[2] An *inspiring vision* resonates with the people working on the product, and it provides motivation and guidance even if the going gets tough.

A *concise vision*, finally, is easy to communicate and understand. To achieve this, I like to capture the vision as a slogan—a short, memorable phrase such as "help people eat healthily." A powerful exercise is to ask the key stakeholders to formulate their visions for the product and to share them with one another. Then look for common ground and use it to create a big, shared, inspiring, and concise vision.

---

2   James Kouzes and Barry Posner (2012) describe a shared vision as one of five core leadership practices.

Find Out How Vision, Strategy, and Tactics Relate

As powerful as they are, the vision and the product strategy are not enough to create a successful product. What's missing are the tactics—the details required to develop a great product, including the user stories and the design sketches. Figure 4 shows how the vision guides the product strategy and how the strategy directs the tactics.

FIGURE 4: Vision, Strategy, and Tactics

Without a valid product strategy—a strategy that has been validated and does not contain any significant risks—you will struggle to discover the right product details; to create the right epics, user stories, story maps, scenarios, design sketches, and mock-ups; and to make the right architecture and technology decisions. If you are not clear on the path, then how can you take the right steps?

But it's not only the strategy that shapes the tactics. The latter also influences the former. As you collect data about how people respond to your product, you learn more about the customer needs and how best to address them. This may require smaller strategy updates, but it could also result in bigger changes, such as pivoting or sun-setting your product: significantly changing your strategy or phasing out the product, respectively. Think of YouTube, which pivoted from a video-dating to a video-sharing site; or take Google Buzz, a social networking, microblogging, and messaging tool, which was taken off the market a year after its introduction in 2010 due to its lack of success. Similarly, if you struggle to find a valid strategy, then this could indicate that your vision is a hazy, unattainable dream that you should wake up from. Vision, strategy, and tactics hence influence one another. Table 1 provides an overview of the three concepts, together with sample artifacts.

TABLE 1: Vision, Strategy, and Tactics

Level	Description	Sample Artifacts
Vision	Describes the positive change the product should bring about, and answers *why* the product should exist. Guides the strategy.	Vision statement or slogan.
Strategy	States the path for attaining the vision; captures *how* the vision should be realized; directs the tactics.	Product strategy, product roadmap, business model.
Tactics	Describes the steps along the way, and the details required to develop a successful product. May lead to strategy changes.	Product backlog, epics, user stories, story maps, scenarios, interaction and workflow diagrams, design sketches, mock-ups, architecture model.

Let the Business Strategy Guide the Product Strategy

A product is a means to an end. By benefiting its customers and users, it should create value for your company. It is therefore important that your product strategy supports the overall business strategy. A business strategy describes how your company wants to achieve its overall objectives. It determines, for instance, which new innovation initiatives your company invests in, which markets you target, which role organic growth and acquisitions play, and how your company sets itself apart from the competition. Take Apple and Samsung, two companies that have employed different business strategies in the same marketplace. At the time of writing, Apple releases a few high-end and highly priced products while Samsung focuses on capturing market share with a wide range of offerings. Some companies refer to their business strategy as the company mission. When I worked at Intel in the late 1990s, the company mission was to "be the preeminent building block supplier to the worldwide Internet economy."[3]

---

3   Intel's mission statement of the year 2000.

To ensure that your product helps the company move in the right direction and that your strategy receives the necessary support from management and stakeholders, the business strategy has to direct the product strategy, as Figure 5 shows. Similarly, your overall company vision should influence the vision of your product.

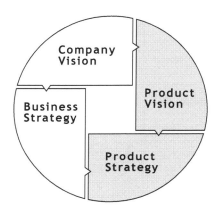

FIGURE 5: Business and Product Strategy

To put it a different way, the product vision should be in line with the overall company vision, and the product strategy should help implement the business strategy. If your business does not have an overall strategy, or if you are unaware of what it is, then delay formulating a product strategy until a business strategy becomes available—unless you work for a start-up, in which case your business and product strategy are likely to be identical.

Be Clear on Your Innovation Strategy

Products are value-creating vehicles. In order to generate value, a product has to offer something new; it has to innovate to a greater or lesser extent. Innovations range from small incremental steps, such as improving the user experience for an existing product, to big and bold ones—think of the original iPhone, the Nintendo Wii, or the Uber taxi service. It's important to understand which innovation strategy your product executes and which innovation type it represents, as this will shape the product strategy. A helpful way to classify innovations is the Innovation Ambition Matrix developed by Bansi Nagji and Geoff Tuff and shown in Figure 6.[4]

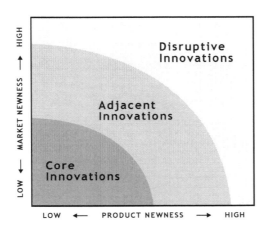

FIGURE 6: The Innovation Ambition Matrix

The matrix in Figure 6 considers the newness of the product on the horizontal axis and the newness of the market on the vertical axis. This allows us to distinguish three different innovation types: core, adjacent, and disruptive.[5]

---

4   Note that I use the term *disruptive* instead of *transformational*, which Nagji and Tuff (2012) employed. Some people use *incremental* instead of *core*, *evolutionary* for *adjacent*, and *revolutionary* or *breakthrough* for *disruptive*.

5   The Innovation Ambition Matrix is based on the Ansoff matrix, which explores the relationship between the product and the market; it distinguishes an existing product from a new product and an existing market from a new one. This gives rise to four growth strategies: market penetration, product development, market development, and diversification. *Market penetration* means incrementally enhancing an existing product to increase its market share. *Product development* involves creating a new product for an existing market—a market you already serve. *Market development* refers to entering a market that's new to your company with an existing product. *Diversification* implies developing a new product for a new market (Ansoff, 1957).

Core Innovations

Core innovations optimize existing products for established markets; they draw on the skills and assets your company already has in place, and they make incremental changes to current products. These initiatives are core to your business, as they generate today's revenues. Most of your company's products are likely to belong to this category (unless you work for a start-up). Examples of core innovations include Microsoft's Windows operating system and the Office suite. Both are major revenue sources for the company. The longer-term growth potential of core products is low, and so is the amount of risk and uncertainty present. Your ability to create a reliable financial forecast or business case is high due to your in-depth knowledge of the market and the product. Because core products leverage existing assets, a conservative attitude is appropriate. You should aim to protect the product, focus on operational excellence, avoid mistakes, optimize the existing business model, and use proven technologies—unless you decide to make a bigger change to your product, such as taking it to a new market, which would turn it into an *adjacent innovation*.

Adjacent Innovations

Adjacent innovations involve leveraging something your company does well into a new space—for example, taking an existing product to a market that's new to the company or creating a new product for an existing market. Examples of the former include Microsoft entering the server market with Windows NT in 1993 and Facebook moving into the online payment space with its Messenger application.[6] Examples of the latter include the Apple TV and Google's Chrome browser. Both companies entered an existing market (TV set-top boxes and web browsers, respectively) with a new product. Adjacent innovations allow you to open up new revenue sources, but they require fresh insights

---

6   Facebook added a "send money" feature to its Messenger product in March 2015. For more information, see http://newsroom.fb.com/news/2015/03/send-money-to-friends-in-messenger/

into customer needs, demand trends, market structure, competitive dynamics, technologies, and other market variables. You may also have to acquire new skills, use new technologies, and adapt an existing business model. The amount of risk and uncertainty present is therefore considerably higher than in core innovations. It consequently requires more time to develop a valid product strategy, and it becomes difficult to create a reliable financial forecast. To succeed with adjacent innovation, you should adopt an inquisitive attitude, be willing to take informed risks, and have the ability to make mistakes and fail. You will benefit from having a dedicated, collocated product team that is loosely coupled to the rest of the organization and that applies agile and lean product development practices.

Disruptive Innovations

Core and adjacent innovations provide you with the benefit of leveraging existing skills and assets, both intellectual and material. This makes the challenge of innovating successfully manageable.[7] Unfortunately, such innovations also share a significant disadvantage: they address an existing market, and their growth prospects are limited by your ability to grow the market and capture more market share—that is, to attract more customers and users. In order to experience higher long-term growth, your company should invest in disruptive innovations. Apple, for instance, disrupted the mobile-phone market with the iPhone by offering a product with superior usability, as well as better design and better mobile Internet; Nintendo disrupted the games-console market with its Wii, which could be used without a traditional control or keyboard and was offered at a lower price; Amazon disrupted the retail book market with its online platform, making it easier and more convenient for consumers to shop, and offering greater choice and lower prices. While disruptive products often use disruptive technologies—for example, the touch screen in the case

---

7   C. M. Christensen (1997) refers to core and adjacent innovations as *sustaining*, as they address established markets and build on existing assets.

of the iPhone, and the Internet in the case of Amazon—a disruptive technology does not necessarily create a disruptive innovation. Instead, a disruptive innovation typically solves a customer problem in a better, more convenient, or cheaper way than existing alternatives. A disruptive product also creates a new market by addressing non-consumption: it attracts people who did not take advantage of similar products. But as the disruptive product matures, it makes inroads into an established market, reconstructs market boundaries, and disrupts the market. Take the iPhone as an example. The incumbents, including Nokia and BlackBerry, did not perceive the original iPhone to be a threat; its business features, such as e-mail integration, were too weak. But as the iPhone improved and offered an increasing range of business and productivity apps, more and more people began to use the product, and the market share of Nokia and BlackBerry phones started to decline. The first iPhone also removed the traditional distinction between business and consumer segments, thereby changing the market boundaries.

While disruptive innovations are crucial for enabling future growth and securing the long-term prosperity of your business, most established companies struggle to leverage such innovations effectively. To achieve disruption and to do different things, a company has to do things differently and therefore disrupt itself—at least to a certain extent. It has to discontinue some of the practices that have helped it succeed in its established markets, acquire new skills, find new business models, and often embrace—and in some cases develop—new technologies, such as the touch screen for the iPhone and the motion controller for the Wii. The effort to create a valid product strategy is significantly higher than for adjacent innovations; it may take you several months to find a product that is beneficial, technically feasible, and economically viable.

Succeeding with disruptive innovations requires an entrepreneurial mind-set and the ability to experiment, to make mistakes, and to fail. You will benefit from using an *incubator*: a new, temporary business unit that provides the necessary autonomy to think outside the box, break with traditions, and to iterate and fail quickly. Having a small, collocated team with full-time members is a must, as is employing agile and lean product development practices. Be aware that creating a reliable financial forecast is impossible for disruptive innovations. Requiring a solid business case can prevent you from creating disruptive products. It's often better to use the risk of inaction—the danger of not investing in a disruptive product and therefore losing out on future revenue and profits.[8]

Summary

Table 2 summarizes the three innovation types; it shows that you should adopt different practices and manage products differently depending on their innovation types.

Note that over time, successful disruptive and adjacent products turn into core ones. A good example is the iPhone. While the first version was a disruptive innovation, it has become a major revenue source for Apple. But you can also move a core product into the adjacent space by taking it to a new market. Think of the iPhone 5C, which was aimed at a younger audience and emergent markets. The bottom line is: to grow organically, companies have to continually look for new growth opportunities and invest in adjacent and disruptive products—the products that generate tomorrow's cash.

---

8   Nagji and Tuff (2012) recommend that companies should invest at least 10 percent in disruptive innovations.

TABLE 2: The Three Innovation Types and Their Impact

Areas	Core Innovation	Adjacent Innovation	Disruptive Innovation
Product	Optimize an existing product for an established market.	Create a new product for an existing market, or take an existing product to a market that's new to the company.	Create both a new product and a new market.
Growth Potential and Risk	Low	Medium	High
Attitude	Conservative—protect existing assets, focus on operational excellence; avoid mistakes; optimize existing business models.	Inquisitive—take informed risks; look for new growth opportunities while leveraging existing skills, assets, and business models.	Entrepreneurial—create new assets, develop new skills, and find a valid business model. Mistakes and failure are unavoidable.
Organization	Business as usual; matrix organization.	Dedicated, collocated product team that is loosely coupled to the rest of the organization.	Incubator with a small, full-time product team that is autonomous and collocated.
Technologies	Proven technologies; changes usually result in incremental improvements.	New technologies may be necessary to gain a competitive advantage.	New, disruptive technologies are likely to be required.
Research and Validation Effort	Low (hours to days)	Medium (weeks)	High (months)
Reliable Financial Forecast	Possible	Difficult to create	Impossible to create

Take Advantage of the Product Life Cycle Model

The purpose of the product strategy is to maximize the chances of achieving product success: to ensure that your product grows and prospers. A helpful model to understand how products develop over time is the product life cycle. The idea behind the life cycle model is simple. Like a living being, a product is born or launched; it then develops, grows, and matures. At some point it declines, and eventually the product dies and is taken off the market, as Figure 7 shows.[9]

---

9   Theodore Levitt (1965) first described the product life cycle model in his article "Exploit the Product Life Cycle." You can find a comprehensive discussion of the product life cycle in Baker and Hart (2007).

The product life cycle model in Figure 7 presents five stages: development, introduction, growth, maturity, and decline. I have also added three important events in the life of a product: launch, when the product first becomes available; achieving product-market fit (PMF), when your product is ready to serve the mainstream market; and end of life, when you decide to discontinue your product. Of the five stages, growth and maturity are the most attractive ones, as they provide you with the biggest business benefits. For revenue-generating products, your product should become profitable around PMF, and it should offer the highest profit margin in maturity. You should therefore aim to get your product into the growth stage quickly, and to keep it there for as long as you can.

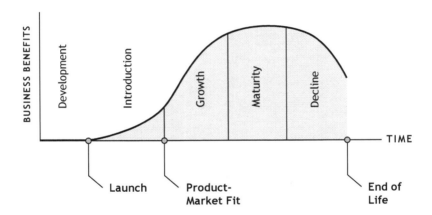

FIGURE 7: The Product Life Cycle Model

While the curve in Figure 7 is roughly bell-shaped, your product's actual trajectory may differ significantly: it may be steeper or flatter. This demonstrates that the life cycle model is not a predictive tool that forecasts the business benefits your product will generate. Instead, it is a sense-making model that helps you reflect on how your product is doing so you can make the right strategic decisions. In order to leverage the product life cycle model, you have to define the business benefits your product delivers and then track them over time. For revenue-generating products, for example, revenue is commonly used, but if your product exists to sell another product or service, then the number of active users might be the appropriate metric to track.

As an example let's take a look at a sample product life cycle curve. Figure 8 illustrates the life cycle of the iPod family by showing iPod sales per year.

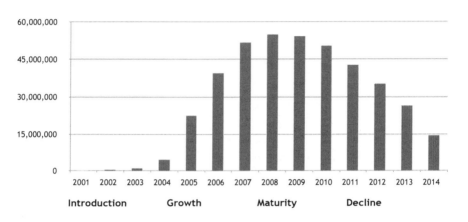

FIGURE 8: The Life Cycle of the iPod Family[10]

As Figure 8 shows, the iPod was launched in 2001 as Apple's first consumer music gadget. The company was a new entrant in the digital-music-player market, which at the time was dominated by products like the Nomad Jukebox from Creative Labs. In 2002, the iPod became Windows-compatible, and sales subsequently reached 600,000 units. In the following year, Apple launched iTunes, which helped sell more than 900,000 units in 2003 and nearly 4.5 million in 2004. The iPod had entered the growth stage and become the dominant digital-music player in the United States. To sustain growth, Apple enhanced the product and added new features, for instance, the ability to show photos and videos. The company also introduced new product variants,

---

10   The sources for the data shown in the graph include
   • https://commons.wikimedia.org/wiki/File%3AIpod_sales_per_quarter.svg
   • statista.com/statistics/276307/global-apple-ipod-sales-since-fiscal-year-2006/
   • apple.com/pr/products/ipodhistory/.

such as the iPod Nano and iPod shuffle in 2005 and the iPod Touch in 2007. Additionally, Apple issued a number of limited iPod editions, including a black-and-red U2 special edition. Sales of the iPod reached their peak in 2008, which also marked the product's maturity stage. In 2009, iPod sales started to decline. As a consequence, Apple discontinued the original iPod, now called the iPod Classic, in 2014.

Development

Let's now look at the individual life cycle stages and how they influence the product strategy. Before the launch your primary goal is to find a valid product strategy—a strategy that results in a product that is beneficial, feasible, and economically viable.[11] In this period you are likely to carry out some research and validation work, and you may have to pivot—that is, to significantly change your strategy and choose a different path for attaining your vision. Take, for example, the idea mentioned earlier of creating a healthy-eating app. If it turns out that building an app is not a valid approach, I could pivot and choose to write a book on healthy eating instead.

Don't make the mistake of trying to launch the perfect product. No product is impeccable from day one. Even iconic products like the iPhone had a comparatively humble start. Think of all the things the very first iPhone could not do: no videos, no copy and paste, and no third-party apps—just to name just a few. The trick is therefore to launch a *good-enough* product, a product that does a good job of meeting the primary customer need, and to subsequently adapt and enhance it. How good your initial product has to be is closely linked with its innovation type. The initial version of a disruptive product can be comparatively basic, like the original iPhone. An adjacent product, however, faces higher customer expectations, as it addresses an established market where the customers have viable alternatives to choose from. Take the Google Chrome browser as an example. When the product was launched in 2008, the company entered an existing market with a

---

11 Ries (2011) calls such a strategy a *validated* strategy.

number of established products, including Internet Explorer, Firefox, Opera, and Safari. In order to succeed, Google had to offer a product that was faster, more secure, and simpler to use than the competing browsers. The company also heavily advertised its product, for instance by using poster ads at train stations in London.

Introduction

After the launch your objective is to achieve PMF and to experience growth as quickly as possible. How long this is likely to take you and how much effort it will require, depends on your product's innovation type. Building an initial customer base and finding out if and how people use the product is particularly important for disruptive innovations. Take Twitter as an example. The company had to discover how people used the product to decide how to move it forward, as Twitter's cofounder Ev Williams explains: "With Twitter, it wasn't clear what it was... Twitter actually changed from what we thought it was in the beginning, which we described as status updates and a social utility. The insight we eventually came to was [that] Twitter was really more of an information network than it is a social network. That led to all kinds of design decisions, such as the inclusion of search and hash tags and the way retweets work" (Lapowsky 2013). Adjacent products, however, tend to require a shorter introduction stage, as they address an existing market and compete with established products. You can therefore usually learn about the customer and user needs and how best to address them during the research and validation work you do in the development stage.

With both disruptive and adjacent products, make sure you track the product performance and monitor how your product's business benefits develop. If they are flat or rise only slowly, then you should investigate why the uptake is poor. Consider changing your product, or even killing it. The former may entail enhancing or adding features, or it can require a more drastic change, such as pivoting or unbundling the product. Flickr, for example, changed from an online role-playing game to a photo-sharing website; YouTube evolved from a video-dating site to a video-sharing product (Love 2011). While killing your product may sound rather drastic, it frees up resources and avoids investing time, money, and energy on a product that is not going to be successful. Take, for instance, Google Wave, a product that combined e-mail, instant messaging, and wikis. Due to its lack of success, Wave was discontinued at the introduction stage about a year after its launch in 2009.[12] Remember that failure is part and parcel of the innovation process; there is no guarantee that your product will make it to the growth stage and become a success.

If you see a positive market response to your newly launched product, then don't make the mistake of overoptimizing your product for the early market. The initial customers and users of a new tech product are usually happy to put up with a few teething issues as long as they will gain an advantage from using it. To get into the mainstream market, you have to satisfy much higher expectations; you have to provide a product that works flawlessly and is easy to obtain, install, and update. As a consequence, the transition to the growth stage may not be a small, incremental step. Instead, your product may face a gap or chasm between the early and the mainstream market that you have to overcome (Moore 2006). Figure 9 shows the product life cycle with such a chasm between the introduction and the growth stage.

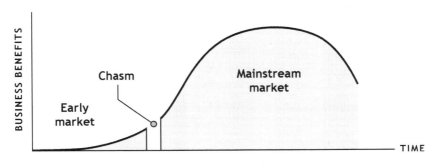

FIGURE 9: The Product Life Cycle with Chasm

---

12 Google has released most of Wave's source code to the Apache Software Foundation: https://en.wikipedia.org/wiki/Apache_Wave and http://incubator.apache.org/wave/about.html.

To bridge the chasm, you have to adapt and improve your product. This may include enhancing the user experience, adding or improving features, or refactoring the architecture to increase performance and stability.[13] In addition, you may have to adjust the business model and revisit, for example, the cost of acquiring customers and the marketing and sales channels you use. The size of the chasm is influenced by your product's innovation type. While the initial version of a disruptive product can be simpler and more basic than an adjacent one, it tends to require more time and effort to achieve PMF and experience growth. An adjacent product usually faces a smaller gap between the introduction and the growth stage, as the initial expectations for the product are typically higher.

Growth

Once you start to experience significant growth, you have achieved PMF. You should now have a product that fits the market and does a good job of creating value for the mainstream customers and users and for your business.[14] For a revenue-generating product, you should have reached the break-even point by now and should be benefiting from a positive cash flow. Your strategy now needs to focus on penetrating the market, sustaining the growth, and fending off competitors. Therefore, you have to find ways to attract more customers and users and clearly differentiate your product, since competitors may start to copy some of its features. At the same time, you have to manage the growth and deal with a product that serves an ever-growing audience, is becoming increasingly feature-rich, and requires more and more people to develop it. You may want to start unbundling your product and promote

---

13 An *architecture refactoring* is a larger refactoring exercise that addresses not only individual classes and methods, but also the overall structure of a software product. While class-level refactoring should be part of the normal development work, architecture refactoring often requires a dedicated effort, such as a whole sprint or even an entire release.

14 Downes and Nunes (2013) suggest that certain disruptions only have two customer groups: *trial users* and *the vast majority*. The former roughly correspond to the early market and the latter to the mainstream market.

features to products in their own right, or you could employ product variants. (I explain both techniques later in this part.)

Maturity, Life Cycle Extension, and Decline

As your product matures, growth will eventually start to stagnate. When this happens, you face an important strategic inflection point. One option is to accept your product's trajectory, let it continue to mature, and keep it at this stage for as long as possible by, for instance, defending its market share and reducing cost. Alternatively, you can move the product back into the growth stage thereby extending its life cycle, as Figure 10 shows.[15]

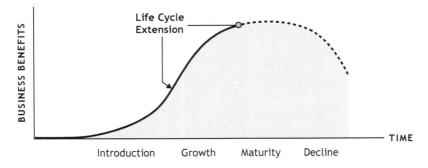

FIGURE 10: Extending the Product Life Cycle

A number of techniques can help you make an aging product attractive again including enhancing its capabilities and adding new features. Take the iPod Classic mentioned earlier. Apple made considerable changes to the product throughout its life cycle: it decreased its weight, extended the battery life, and added the ability to view photos and watch videos, to name just a few. Sometimes, though, the opposite strategy is more appropriate, and instead of adding you may want to remove features and declutter your product. Microsoft Word is another example. Microsoft has made significant efforts to simplify the application in recent years, thereby improving

---

15 Moon (2005) argues that the product life cycle does not have to be linear, and that rejuvenating the product can be a great option.

the user experience and making it easier for people to use the product. Another way to stimulate growth is to take your product to a new market or market segment, thereby turning it into an adjacent innovation. Apple, for example, introduced the iPhone 5C in 2013 to target a younger audience and emerging markets. Finally, you might consider bundling your product with other offerings to increase its attractiveness. For instance, mobile operators in the United Kingdom have started to offer free streaming subscriptions when customers purchase higher-priced contracts.

Despite your best efforts, your product will one day reach the decline stage. During this stage, you want to milk it for long as you can while minimizing the investment that goes into the product. As the profits it generates start dropping, you should consider discontinuing it—just as Apple did with the iPod Classic in 2014.

Summary

Table 3 summarizes how the life cycle stages shape the product strategy.

TABLE 3: The Product Life Cycle and the Product Strategy

Life Cycle Stage	Strategy
Development	Develop a valid strategy: a strategy that results in a product that is beneficial, feasible, and economically viable.
Introduction	Adapt and improve your product to achieve product-market fit (PMF). This may require incremental changes such as improving the customer experience, adding new features, and refactoring the architecture. But it may also make a more drastic change or pivot necessary. Aim to achieve the break-even point for a revenue-generating product by the end of this stage. Ensure that your business model is scalable.
Growth	Sustain the growth by penetrating the market and fending off competitors. Keep your product attractive, and refine it. Manage the growth by unbundling your product or by creating variants, for instance. Ensure that your product is profitable (if it is meant to generate revenue).
Maturity	As growth stagnates, extend the life cycle and revive growth by taking the product to a new market, for example, or bundling it with another product or service. Alternatively, milk your product by serving the late majority. Defend its market share and focus on profitability for revenue-generating products.
Decline	Reduce cost to keep the product profitable for as long as possible, then start phasing it out.

As Table 3 shows, the strategy for a new product should first help you get to launch, then to achieve PMF, and then to sustain the growth. Once the growth starts to stagnate, you have reached an important strategic inflection point: You either revitalize your product, for instance, by taking it to a new market, or you let it mature and eventually decline and die. As you have probably noticed, the strategic work does not end until you discontinue your product. You should therefore regularly assess your product's performance and adjust your strategy accordingly. Strategy and execution go hand in hand for digital products. They are two sides of the same coin.

Capture Your Strategy with the Product Vision Board

Even the best strategy is useless if you can't communicate it effectively. The Product Vision Board is a simple yet powerful tool that helps you with this. I have designed it to describe, communicate, test, correct, and refine the product strategy.

The Product Vision Board consists of the five sections shown in Figure 11. The top section captures the vision; the bottom four sections describe the product strategy.

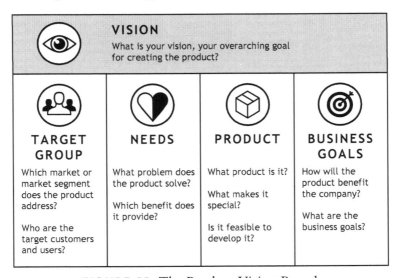

FIGURE 11: The Product Vision Board

The top section in Figure 11 is called *Vision*. It captures your overarching goal, which is expressed as a brief vision statement or slogan. The leftmost bottom section is called *Target Group*. It describes your market or market segment, the customers, and the users. The next section is called *Needs*, which states the value the product creates for your target group, the problem that the product solves, or the benefit it provides. The *Product* section captures the actual product; it explains what makes your product special and why it stands out. It also asks whether it is feasible for your organization to develop the product. The last section, titled *Business Goals*, captures the desired business benefits—the value the product should create for your company. Examples include opening up a new revenue source, achieving a profitability target, reducing cost, or being able to provide a service or sell another product. There is also an extended version of the Product Vision Board with additional sections to capture the business model, which I discuss below.

When you create your Product Vision Board, start with your vision, and then describe your strategy by filling in the bottom sections. You can use the Product Vision Board to describe the vision and strategy for a brand-new product or for an existing one. In the latter case, you may want to invite the stakeholders and ask them to create their personal Product Vision Boards. Then compare the results and see whether there is a shared vision and a shared product strategy; if not, determine where the main differences are and decide how to address them.

You can download the Product Vision Board template from my website, www.romanpichler.com, where you can also find more information about the tool. Alternatively, you may choose to re-create it using your favorite tool—be it an electronic spreadsheet or a whiteboard. A number of other tools are also available to capture the product strategy, of course, including the Lean Canvas (Maurya 2012) and the Business Model Canvas (Osterwalder and Pigneur 2010). Choose the one that works best for you.

Complement Your Strategy with a Business Model

It's great to determine the market segment, the value proposition, and the business goals of your product. But you should also understand how to reach the desired business benefits stated in your strategy, and how you can monetize your product—be it by selling it or by using it to sell another product or service. In other words, you should complement your product strategy with a business model.

Common Business Models

Common business models for digital products include subscription, freemium, advertising, and bait and hook. A *subscription* business model requires customers to pay a subscription price to access the product, as is the case for Microsoft Office and Adobe Photoshop. *Freemium* means giving away a basic version for free but charging for premium features, as Spotify and Skype do. *Advertising* generates revenue from in-app or online ads—a business model employed, for example, by YouTube, Facebook, and many news websites. *Bait and hook* provides a free or discounted product and generates revenue from selling another product or service that locks in the customer. Take, for instance, iTunes: while the product itself is free, it is only truly useful when combined with a comparatively expensive iPod, iPhone, or iPad. Once you have started using Apple products, you are locked into the Apple ecosystem.

Capturing the Business Model

For some products, the business model already exists, as in the case of iTunes. The product was created to execute an existing business model and to help sell iPods. But for other products, such as Facebook and Twitter, the product and the business model are created together. Among the various tools available to describe your business model, the Business Model Canvas (Osterwalder and Pigneur 2010) is probably the most well known. But if the Product Vision Board described earlier resonates with you, then you can simply extend the board and describe your business model alongside the vision and the product strategy, as Figure 12 shows. I find this option especially attractive when the product and business model are developed together.

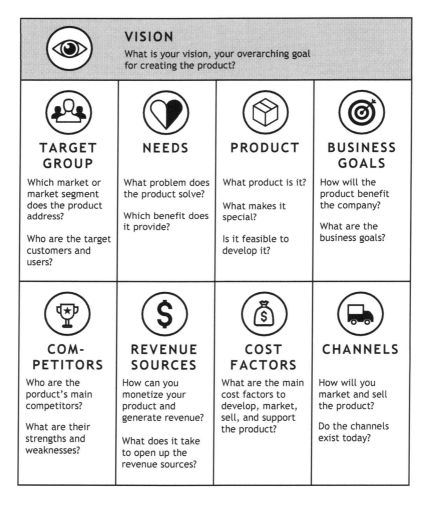

FIGURE 12: The Extended Product Vision Board

The first and second rows of the board in Figure 12 are identical to the standard Product Vision Board. The business model is captured in the bottom row, which is inspired by the Business Model Canvas and provides the following four sections:

- *Competitors* describes the strengths and weaknesses of the competition and their products. It uses your insights from performing a competitor analysis and helps ensure that your product stands out.
- *Revenue Sources* captures the way your product generates money: for instance, by selling licenses, subscriptions, or online or in-app ads, or by charging for premium features.
- *Cost Factors* states the cost incurred by developing, marketing, selling, and supporting your product. This includes the cost of acquiring users and customers, purchasing third-party components, and paying for the services and products provided by partners and suppliers.
- *Channels* are the ways you will contact your users and customers to inform them about your product and to sell and deliver the product. The latter can range from implementing the requirements of an online app store to working with retailers to get some shelf space for a shrink-wrapped product. Consider if the appropriate sales and marketing channels already exist, or if you have to create or acquire them.

You can download the Extended Vision Board for free from my website, where more information on the tool is available.

Business Model vs. Business Case

The business model explains how the product is monetized, but it does not quantify the revenue generated or the cost incurred. That's done by a business case, which forecasts the product's financial performance, typically over the next two to three years. This allows you to judge if developing and providing the product is an attractive investment, and it helps you anticipate the cash flow. Depending on your product's innovation type, a *realistic* business case can be challenging to create, as discussed earlier. For core products, creating such a business case is usually feasible; for adjacent products, it can be very hard; for disruptive products, it is impossible, as the market for your product does not exist yet. For adjacent and particularly disruptive products, you should consider using the business model to justify the investment, together with the inaction risk—that is, for example, the loss that would materialize if the product were not developed and the related business benefits were not realized.

Choose the Right Key Performance Indicators (KPIs) for Your Product

Key performance indicators (KPIs) are metrics that measure your product's performance. They help you understand if the product is meetings its business goals, and if the product strategy is working. Without KPIs, you end up guessing how well your product is performing. It's like driving with your vision blurred: You can't see if you are heading in the right direction or getting closer to your destination. You may have a hunch or intuition, but how can you tell that it's right? Using KPIs and collecting the right data helps you balance opinions, beliefs, and gut feelings with empirical evidence, which increases the chances of making the right decisions and providing a successful product. This section helps you choose the right indicators for your product.

Making the Business Goals Measurable

In order to choose the right KPIs, use the business goals stated in the product strategy. For example, if your product directly generates revenue, then revenue is likely to be a key indicator. But knowing the business goals is not enough. To effectively apply the indicators, analyze the data you collect, and take the right actions, the goals must be *measurable*. Say my company decided to invest in creating a healthy-eating app mentioned earlier, with the goal of diversifying the business and opening up a new revenue source. While this might be a good idea, the goal is not specific enough. I can't tell if the product is making enough revenue and meeting its business goal; there is no target and no time frame stated that I can use to measure progress against. The challenge is to establish a measurable goal that's also *realistic,* particularly for brand-new and young products, whose business benefits are difficult to correctly quantify.

One helpful technique for addressing this challenge is to work with ratios and ranges (Croll and Yoskovitz 2013). Instead of stating that the new product should create x amount of revenue per year, I could say, for instance, that the product should increase the company's revenue by 5 to 10 percent within one year after its launch, for instance. While this goal might still be unrealistic, I have at least drawn a line in the sand that progress can be measured against. If it turns out that the goal is too ambitious, you should recognize this, move the line, and adjust your target. The good news is that the longer you work with your product and the more stable it becomes, the easier it gets to come up with measurable goals that can actually be met. With measurable business goals in place, follow the tips below to find the right performance indicators for your product.

Choosing Relevant Indicators

Avoid vanity metrics, which are measures that make your product look good but don't add value (Ries 2009). Take the number of downloads for my healthy-eating app as an example. While a fair number of people might download the app, this tells me little about how successful it is. Instead, it indicates the effectiveness of my marketing efforts. Rather than measuring downloads, I should choose a relevant and helpful metric, such as daily active usage or referral rate. Whenever you select an indicator, check if the indicator actually measures performance or just makes your product look good.

Don't measure everything that can be measured, and don't blindly trust an analytics tool to collect the right data. Instead, use the business goals to choose a small number of metrics that truly help you understand how your product performs. Otherwise, you take the risk of wasting time and effort analyzing data that provides little or no value. In the worst case, you act on irrelevant data and make the wrong decisions. Think of driving a car. A small number of indicators are helpful for getting to your destination, including speed, fuel consumption, and revolutions per minute. If the car dashboard always showed other data, such as oil pressure or battery status, it would be harder to take in the relevant information.

In addition, be aware that some metrics are sensitive to the product life cycle. You usually cannot measure profit, for example, before your products enters the growth stage.[16] And tracking adoption rate and referrals is very useful in the introduction and growth stages, but it is less so in the maturity and decline stages.

Quantitative and Qualitative KPIs

As their name suggests, quantitative indicators, such as daily active users or revenue, measure the quantity of something rather than its quality. This has the benefit of collecting "hard" and statistically representative data. Qualitative indicators, such as user feedback, help you understand *why* something has happened—for instance, why users aren't as satisfied with the product as expected. Combining the two types gives you a balanced outlook on how your product is doing. Doing so reduces the risk of losing sight of the most important success factor: the people behind the numbers—that is, the individuals who buy and use the product.

Lagging and Leading Indicators

Lagging indicators, such as revenue, profit, and cost, are backward-focused and tell you about the outcome of past actions. Leading indicators, in contrast, help you understand how likely it is that your product will meet a goal in the future. Take product quality as an example. If the code is becoming increasingly complex, then adding new features will become more expensive, and meeting a profit target will become harder. Using both backward- and forward-focused indicators tells you if you have met the business goals and helps you anticipate if the product is likely to meet future goals.

---

16 A revenue-generating product typically achieves the break-even point at the transition from the introduction to the growth stage.

Looking beyond Financial and Customer Indicators

Financial indicators, such as revenue and profit, and customer metrics, like engagement and referral rates, are the two most common indicator types in my experience. While these metrics are undoubtedly important, they are not sufficient. Say your product is meeting its revenue and profit goals, and customer engagement and referral rates are high. This suggests that your product is doing well; there is no reason to worry. But if at the same time the team motivation is low or the code quality is deteriorating, you should still be concerned. These indicators suggest that achieving product success will be much harder in the future. You should therefore look beyond financial and customer indicators and also use the relevant product, process, and people indicators. This creates a holistic outlook on the product performance, and it reduces the risk that you miss important warning signs.[17]

Leveraging Trends

Compare the data you analyze to other time periods, for example, user groups, competitors, and cancellation rates from quarter to quarter, or revenue growth over the last six weeks. This helps you spot trends—for instance, if revenue is increasing, staying flat, or declining. Trends allow you to better understand what's happening and to take the right actions. If a decline in revenue is a one-off occurrence, for instance, there is probably no reason to be overly worried. But if it is a trend, then you should investigate how you can stop and reverse it—unless you are about to sunset your product.

---

17 This does not mean that as the person in charge of the product, you have to collect all the product, process, and people data. The development team and the ScrumMaster should help you gather them. You may want to ask the Scrum-Master, for instance, to collect feedback from the team members about their motivation at the end of the retrospective.

Sample KPIs

To conclude our discussion, let's take a look at some sample KPIs. The measurements in Table 4 are grouped into four perspectives: financial, customer, product and process, and people. The groups are inspired by David Norton and Robert Kaplan's work on balanced scorecards, and I explain in the next section how the groups help you create a product scorecard to effectively track product performance.[18] Please note that the list of indicators is not intended to be complete; it may not contain all the metrics you need, and some measures may not be applicable to your product. Let me stress again that you should only choose those indicators that measure the performance of your product against the business goals.

TABLE 4: Sample Key Performance Indicators

Perspective	Sample KPIs	Brief Description
Financial	Revenue	How much revenue is your product generating?
	Cost	What is the cost of developing and launching major releases or product versions?
	Cost of acquisition	How much does it cost to acquire a customer?
	Profit	How much profit is the product making? Note that you may want to track different profit types, including net and gross profit.
	Customer life-time value	How much profit do individual customers create across the entire future relationship?
	Cash flow	Is the cash flow positive or negative? If negative, when do you expect to reach the break-even point?
Customer	Market share	How big is your market share compared to the competition?
	Adoption rate	Is your product gaining traction in the marketplace? If so, how quickly?
	Engagement	How engaged are the users? How many active daily users does the product have?
	Retention	How many customers are coming back?

---

18 Norton and Kaplan (1996) also distinguish four perspectives, but instead of *product and process* and *people*, they use the terms *internal business processes* and *learning and growth*, respectively.

Perspective	Sample KPIs	Brief Description
Customer	Net promoter score and referrals	How likely is it that people will recommend the product? How many people are actually recommending it?
	Cancellation rate	How many contracts are cancelled?
	Complaints and support requests	How many customer complaints and support queries do you receive? How severe are they?
	Conversation rate	How well are inquiries and evaluations translated into sales?
	Customer and user feedback	Do the customers and users have a positive, neutral, or negative attitude toward your product? What reviews are they providing, what feedback do they submit, and what do they tell you when you talk to them?
Product and Process	User interaction	What are the most and least common user journeys? Where do most drop-offs occur? What are the most and least used features?
	Product quality	Is it easy to change and extend the product? How high are the code complexity and the refactoring potential? How high is the test coverage? How many bugs are found and closed?
	Development process	How effective is the development process? Does it support the work of the team? Does the team have the right environment and the right tools?
	Schedule variances	Do new product versions and major releases meet their objectives? Are they deployed on time and on budget?
People	Team motivation	Is the development team motivated to work on the product? How high are turnover rates and absenteeism?
	Team knowledge and skills	Does the team have the necessary knowledge to do a good job? Does it improve its skills and acquire new knowledge?
	Stakeholder engagement	Do the stakeholders regularly participate in strategy and roadmap reviews and in sprint review meetings?
	Management sponsorship	Do you have the right management sponsor? Is the sponsor interested in the product and its performance?

Track the Product Performance with a Product Scorecard

Once you have selected the right KPIs for your product, you should collect the relevant data and regularly analyze it. A product scorecard or dashboard can help you with this. I like to work with a *balanced* product scorecard that considers the four perspectives listed in Table 4: financial, customer, product and process, and people. This ensures that you take a holistic approach to determining the product performance, and it reduces the risk of overlooking important trends. Figure 13 shows a balanced product scorecard.

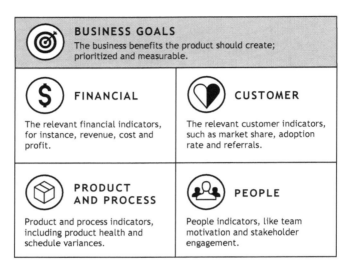

FIGURE 13: Balanced Product Scorecard

The scorecard in Figure 13 is inspired by the work of Norton and Kaplan (1996) on balanced scorecards, which are a business-performance management tool. It states the business goals at the top and the four perspectives underneath. As mentioned in the last section, you should be clear on the business goals your product serves. Prioritize them and ensure that they are measurable. Select only relevant indicators that will help you determine if you are meeting the business goals. If you find the product scorecard in Figure 13 helpful, then download it from my website, where you can find more information about the tool.[19]

Note that the frequency at which the relevant data above becomes available, and how much effort is required to collect it, will vary. Revenue and engagement data, for example, may be collected automatically by your

---

19   The sprint retrospective is a Scrum meeting that improves process and collaboration.

analytics tool, and you may be able to spot relevant changes from one day to the next. But some of the people, product, and process data are not as readily available, and are harder to collect. Take team motivation, for example. If you use the sprint retrospective to gather feedback from the development team to find out how motivated the team members are, the data is collected manually, and it becomes available only once every few weeks. You may therefore find yourself updating the finance and customer perspectives of the product scorecard more often than the other two.

Complement KPIs with Operational Metrics

While KPIs are great for measuring the overall product performance, they are usually not enough. You should consider using additional metrics that complement the KPIs and help you understand how well you are meeting specific product goals—for instance, increasing retention and enhancing the user experience, or making it easier to add new features. I recommend capturing these goals on the product roadmap together with the relevant metrics for measuring when a goal is met (described in more detail in Part 2). In an agile context, product goals are delivered in a stepwise fashion by a number of sprints, which should have their own goals and success criteria. This results in the three-tier goals-and-metrics approach described in Figure 14.

FIGURE 14: Goals and Metrics

As Figure 14 shows, the business goals captured in the product strategy provide the context to identify the right product goals. The latter describe the specific benefits major releases should provide. For example, the goal for the first public release of a new product could be to acquire customers and build a user community (product goals) to eventually generate revenue (business goal). The goals in the roadmap do a similar job for the sprint goals; they help you determine the right objectives of the iterations that build the actual product. The goal of your first sprint could be to test ideas about user interaction or the user interface design. Higher-level goals are therefore progressively broken down into tactical ones, and KPIs are complemented by release and sprint-specific metrics.

If this sounds confusing, then a different example might help. As an avid cyclist, I might choose win an amateur race as my overall goal. After selecting the race, I would identify the training goals required to win the race, for example, increasing my climbing or my sprinting abilities. Next I would break down my training goals into weekly progress goals, such as doing three sessions of interval training. This leads to three different goal levels that are derived from one another but measured individually.

Note that the relationship between the levels in Figure 14 is bidirectional, as the feedback or data generated in a sprint can change the product roadmap. This may in turn have an impact on the product strategy. To build on the cycling example, if my training progress indicates that I cannot win the race, I have to revise my overall goal, select a different race, or be content with a less ambitious result.

Engage the Stakeholders

As brilliant as it may be, your product strategy is useless if the other people involved in making the product a success don't support it. Working with a *shared* strategy is therefore paramount. To achieve this, you should secure the support and buy-in of the stakeholders.

Stakeholder Identification

A stakeholder is anyone who has a stake in your product—anyone who is affected by it or shows an interest in it. While this definition includes customers and users, I use it to refer to the *internal* stakeholders, such as marketing and sales.

In order to identify the stakeholders, ask yourself whose help you need to develop, release, and provide the product. The answer to this question will be specific to your product and company. For a commercial product, the group is likely to include representatives from marketing, sales, support, and management. But it might also comprise people from legal, finance, and human resources. For an in-house product, your stakeholders may be the affected business units, operations, and management.

Stakeholder Analysis and Engagement

Once you have identified the stakeholders, you need to determine how to best engage the individuals. A tool that helps you with this challenge is the Power-Interest Grid, described in Eden and Ackermann (2011). As its name suggests, the grid analyzes the stakeholders by taking into account their power and their interest; it assumes that stakeholders take a low or high interest in your product and have low or high power. This results in four stakeholder groups: *players*, *subjects*, *context setters*, and the *crowd*, as Figure 15 shows. To find out if a stakeholder is likely to be interested in your product, consider if the person will be affected by it; and to understand if a stakeholder has high power, ask yourself if the individual can influence, or even veto, product decisions.

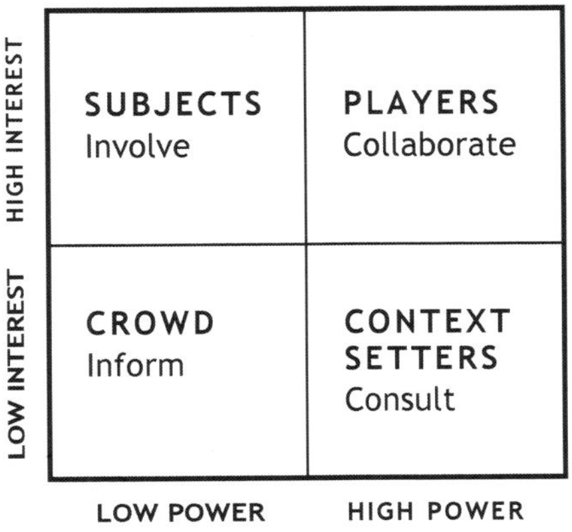

	LOW POWER	HIGH POWER
HIGH INTEREST	**SUBJECTS** Involve	**PLAYERS** Collaborate
LOW INTEREST	**CROWD** Inform	**CONTEXT SETTERS** Consult

FIGURE 15: The Power-Interest Grid

Stakeholders with high interest and high power are called *players*. These individuals are important partners for you; they help you create, validate, and review the product strategy and ideally continue to work with you on the product roadmap. Aim to secure their buy-in, leverage their ideas and knowledge, and establish a close and trustful relationship with them. You should also ensure that these individuals are involved with the product continuously to avoid loss of knowledge and handoffs. It is undesirable, for instance, to have the marketing group send a new representative every time a strategy workshop takes place. Instead, one marketer should represent the group. How closely you should collaborate with the players is influenced by the life cycle stage of your product. I find that close collaboration is particularly important to develop a valid and shared product strategy.

Be aware that *collaboration requires leadership.* As the person in charge of the product, you should be open and collaborative but decisive at the same time. Aim to build consensus with the players, but don't shy away from difficult conversations. Don't settle for the smallest common denominator. Have the courage to make a decision if no agreement can be achieved. Great products are not built on weak compromises. As the saying goes, "A camel is a horse designed by committee."

Subjects are individuals with high interest but low power—for example, product managers and development teams who work on related products. These individuals feel affected by the product and are keen to influence it, but they can't veto or change decisions. Subjects can make great allies who can help you secure understanding and buy-in for your product across the business. Keep them involved by inviting them to bigger strategy-review meetings, for instance, or by sharing ideas with them and asking for their feedback.

People with low interest but high power are called *context setters.* They affect the product's context, but they take little interest in the product itself. Context setters are often powerful senior and executive managers who can make your life difficult if they are not on your side. Regularly consult them to ensure that their opinions are heard—for instance, by having one-on-one meetings. But don't let the context setters intimidate you, and don't allow them to dictate decisions. Be strong and have the courage to say no. Use data and empirical evidence to back up your arguments and convince the context setters.

Everyone else is part of the *crowd*. As these individuals are not particularly interested in your product and don't have the power to influence the product strategy or other product decisions, it's usually sufficient to keep them informed; give them access to the product's wiki website, for instance, or update them on significant strategy changes.

Collaborative Strategy Workshop
Running a collaborative strategy workshop is a great way to create an initial product strategy—be it for a new product or a significant change of an existing one. Invite the players, including members of the development team, to the workshop and consider involving selected subjects, such as product managers of related products. Encourage the workshop attendees to actively contribute to the strategy. Use a tool like the Product Vision Board discussed earlier to structure the conversation and to capture and visualize your ideas. Be aware that the workshop is the first step toward a *valid* product strategy. The objective is not to create a definitive and correct plan of action, but to establish a shared initial strategy. Consider asking the ScrumMaster or a qualified facilitator to set the right tone, establish a trustful and collaborative atmosphere, and facilitate the workshop.

Review and Update the Product Strategy

While a working strategy is key to creating a winning product, it would be a mistake to blindly execute it and assume it will always stay valid. As your product develops and grows, and as the market and the technologies evolve, the product strategy has to change, too. You should therefore regularly review and adjust it. As Winston Churchill put it: "However beautiful the strategy, you should occasionally look at the results." I find four factors to be useful to take into account when re-

viewing the product strategy: the product performance, the competition, the trends, and the company goals and capabilities. Figure 16 illustrates these factors.

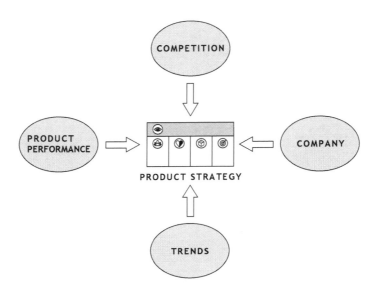

FIGURE 16: Factors Affecting the Strategy

Reflecting on the product's performance using KPIs should help you
understand how successful the product is and if the product is meeting
its business goals. Considering what the competition is doing allows
you to understand if your product is still adequately differentiated, or if
competitors have caught up and are imitating some of its features. Reviewing technology trends and regulatory changes will help you discover opportunities to enhance and future-proof your product. Looking
at your company and any changes in its business strategy will help you
understand if the business goals captured in the product strategy are
still valid. Adapt your strategy appropriately. Be aware that this may
not only mean smaller adjustments but more drastic changes, including
pivoting or even killing the product.

How often you assess the strategy depends on the product maturity and the market volatility. For younger products and dynamic markets, I recommend reviewing the product strategy once per month; for more mature products and markets, perform a strategy check every quarter. Involve the stakeholders—particularly the players—in the review to keep them up-to-date, leverage their knowledge, and secure their buy-in. Align the review of the product strategy with the evaluation of your product roadmap. Any issues in executing the roadmap can indicate that your strategy is no longer valid. Strategy and execution are inter-connected; they form the two sides of the same coin.

STRATEGY DEVELOPMENT

Creating a winning product and ensuring its sustained success is not a matter of luck. It is based on making the right strategic decisions. This chapter discusses a range of product strategy practices to help you make the right choices, such as finding the right audience for your product, making sure your product stands out from the crowd, and bundling and unbundling the product. Let's start with techniques to segment the market and select the right target group.

Segment the Market

Segmenting the market means dividing the potential customers and users into distinct groups. It's like eating cake. Instead of trying to eat the whole cake at once and possibly creating a mess or choking on it, we cut out a neat slice. This allows you to create a focused product with a compelling value proposition and a great user experience. Your segments should be clear-cut so they do not overlap. To put it differently, you should be able to tell who belongs to a segment and who does not. What's more, each segment should be homogenous, and the people within it should respond to your product in the same way.[20] Take my healthy-eating app mentioned earlier. A large group of people could benefit from it, including individuals who want to lose weight and people who have a medical condition like diabetes. Trying to please

---

20 A product focused on a specific segment can help establish a strong brand. Ries and Trout (1994) argue that a brand becomes stronger when you narrow the focus.

everyone would not only be challenging but would also result in a feature-rich product that might not satisfy anyone. Note that segmentation is not only beneficial for developing new products; it also helps you
derive variants from an existing product.

Segmenting by Customer Properties and Benefits

How you segment the market is important. The segments not only define who the customers and users are, but they also influence many
product decisions. While there are different ways to divide up the market, you face two basic choices. You can form segments that are based
on the customer properties, or on the benefits that your product provides. Common customer properties include

- demographics such as age, gender, marital status, occupation,
  education, and income;
- psychographics, including lifestyle, social class, and personality;
- behavioral attributes like usage patterns, attitudes, and brand
  loyalty;
- geographic regions such as Europe, Middle East and Africa
  (EMEA), and Asia-Pacific (APAC);
- industries or verticals—for instance, automotive, education, finance, and health care for business markets, also called business-to-business or B2B; and
- company size, such as small and medium-size enterprises (SMEs)
  for B2B products.

While the attributes listed above differ, they have something important
in common—they all concentrate on the customer, be it a consumer or
a business. Let's use my healthy-eating app again. In order to segment
the market, I could choose demographic and psychographic attributes
and define my target group as men aged 20–30 who are single, work
long hours, don't exercise much, and eat out frequently.

An alternative approach is to divide the market using the benefit the product provides or the problem it addresses (Christensen and
Raynor 2013). This suggests that you first and foremost consider people's needs. For example, if the main benefit of my healthy-eating app

is to help people better understand how much they eat, then there are two groups who may benefit from it: people who would like to lose weight and people who want to better way to determine their calorie intake, such as athletes and people with diabetes. While the first group could contain single men aged 20–30 with poor eating habits, it could equally include married women with young children who want to lose weight but don't have the time or energy to follow a strict diet or exercise regularly. Focusing on the needs and benefits can therefore result in different segments, and consequently a different product.

Choosing the Right Segmentation Approach

But how can you tell which segmentation approach is preferable? Should you segment primarily by customer or by benefit? My answer is simple: look at the innovation type your product represents. Whenever you create an adjacent or disruptive product, segment first by *benefit*. Once you have created your initial benefit-based segments, you can refine them by using appropriate customer properties. In contrast, when your product is a core innovation, divide the market by customer properties, as Figure 17 illustrates.

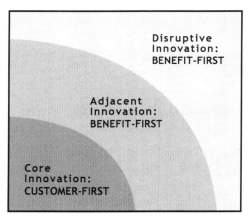

FIGURE 17: Innovation Strategy and Segmentation Approach[21]

---

21   Figure 17 is a version of the Innovation Ambition Matrix described in more detail in the section "Choose the Right Innovation Strategy."

The great thing about benefit-based segmentation is that it reduces the risk of overlooking people who are likely to take advantage of your product; it also offers you the opportunity to reconstruct the market boundaries. Take the Nintendo Wii game console, for instance, which was released in November 2006. Rather than using behavior-based segments such as hard-core and casual gamers and trying to determine how the company could compete in these segments against the likes of Sony PlayStation and Microsoft Xbox, Nintendo looked to the gaming industry's noncustomers and investigated what prevented people from playing video games. This allowed the company to redefine the market boundaries and to connect with older people and young children: two groups that share few demographic and psychographic attributes. The end result was an innovative console that people could interact with in novel ways—through motion control and a magic wand rather than a keyboard or a specialized controller.

Whichever way you segment the market, avoid the following two mistakes: First, don't blindly follow predefined segments. I have seen product managers cling to existing customer-based segments while trying to create new, innovative products. Unsurprisingly, the outcomes were rather poor. Second, don't discard an idea because it does not fit into predefined segments. You may miss opportunities to create a new product or to discover new markets. Take the first iPhone, which launched in 2007, as an example. Apple disregarded the traditional distinction between consumer and business smartphones. Instead, the company created a product that offered "the Internet in your pocket"[22] and appealed to consumers and business users alike.

Pick the Right Segment

Segmenting the market often results in several groups that your product could serve. In the case of my healthy-eating app, I could focus on people who live with diabetes and have to watch what they eat, busy

---

22   Steve Jobs (2015) in his iPhone keynote at Macworld 2007.

mothers who would like to shed a few pounds, or athletes who would like to improve their performance. Addressing all three segments at the same time would be overwhelming. It's therefore a good idea to choose one of them. But which one should I pick? To select the right segment, evaluate the different groups and opt for the most promising one. A great tool to do this is the GE/McKinsey matrix (Coyne 2008). While the matrix was originally developed to assess a business portfolio, it can also be applied to market segments. It encourages you to assess your segments according to their attractiveness and the strength of your business, as Figure 18 shows.

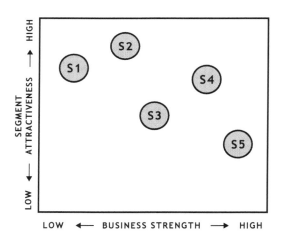

FIGURE 18: GE/McKinsey Matrix

The GE/McKinsey matrix states the attractiveness of the market segment on the vertical axis, and the strength of the business on the horizontal one. It ranks five sample segments according to the two dimensions. The most promising one is S4: it is fairly attractive, and the business has the ability to serve it. S1 and S2 are more attractive than S4, but the business strength is significantly lower. The remaining two segments are less attractive. While the matrix offers a great way to evaluate the segments, the devil is in the details. The effectiveness of the matrix depends on your ability to define what attractiveness and business strength mean. Several criteria may be used to determine how attractive a segment is, including the following:

- Need: How strong is the need, and how much does the group benefit from the product?
- Segment size: How big is it?
- Growth rate: Does it show signs of growth?
- Competitors: Who are the main competitors, and how fierce is the competition?
- Entry barriers: Are there any barriers for entering the segment— for example, high switching or high setup costs?

In order to understand the business strength, investigate your ability to serve the segment. Do you have the necessary skills, knowledge, and expertise to do so? If not, can you acquire them? How difficult and expensive is it to acquire customers? Do you have the right marketing and sales channels in place? If not, what will it take to establish them?

You could spend months collecting the relevant data if you wanted to precisely determine the attractiveness and the business strengths of your product; and if you reconstruct the market boundaries and attempt to disrupt a market, then you cannot gather the relevant information at all. "Markets that don't exist can't be analyzed," as Clayton Christensen put it (1997, p. xxi). I therefore recommend qualitatively evaluating the segments. Perform a quick assessment; spend hours rather than weeks or months and test if you are indeed addressing the right people as part of the strategy-validation effort (explain in more detail later). If it turns out that you have picked the wrong target group, then select and test the next segment. Say that I decide to first address the athlete segment with my shiny new healthy-eating app. I would then validate the segment and carry out some direct observation, problem interviews, and competitor analysis, for instance. If it turns out that the athlete segment does not benefit enough from a dedicated app, I would select and test the next segment—for example, the people with diabetes or the moms who want to lose weight—until I find an attractive segment or decide to pivot.

Use Personas to Describe the Customers and Users

A helpful technique to describe the customers and the users of your product is the use of *personas*.[23] Personas are fictional characters that usually consist of a name and a picture; relevant characteristics, behaviors, and attitudes; and a goal. The goal is the benefit the persona wants to achieve, or the problem the character wants to see solved. Different personas can have different goals. For instance, I could create a persona for my healthy-eating app who wants to lose weight, and another persona who wants to experience fewer digestive problems. Understanding the personas' goals allows you to create a product that does a great job at creating value for the customers and users. It avoids the fallacy of a solution-centric approach: worrying more about the product and its features and technologies than the reason people would want to buy and use it in the first place.

Persona Tips

Any persona description should be based on knowledge gained from direct interaction with the target customers and users. Before you create your personas, you should therefore get to know your audience, for example, by observing how they currently get a job done and by interviewing them. Otherwise, your characters may not accurately represent your target group. In the worst case, they are based on ideas and speculation, not real people. Put aside any ideas about the desired user experience and the product features when you develop your personas. Describe the characters according to your market insights. Do not make them fit your ideas and assumptions!

---

23   Alan Cooper pioneered the use of personas in software development; see Cooper (1999).

Distinguish between customer or buyer personas and user personas, as their goals and characteristics may significantly differ. This is particularly helpful for B2B products like enterprise software or healthcare equipment. Take a medical device like an X-ray machine. While the radiologists who use the machine will want to create accurate diagnoses, a hospital trust that purchases the machine is likely to have a different goal: a low total cost of ownership.

Once you have created a cast of characters, select a *primary persona*. This is the persona you mainly develop the product for. Working with a primary persona creates focus and facilitates decision making: the goal of the primary persona should largely determine the user experience (UX) and the product's functionality. If you find it difficult to choose one primary persona, this may indicate that your target market is too large and heterogeneous, or that your product has become too big and complex. If that's the case, then resegment the market, unbundle your product, or introduce product variants.

Finally, visualize your personas. Put them on the office wall so they are visible to the development team. Some of my clients even print out personas on life-size cardboard sheets. Seeing the personas reminds the development-team members who they are designing and building the software for, and it avoids a solution-centric mind-set.

A Persona Template

To help you create your persona descriptions, I have developed a simple but powerful template that you can download from my website. The persona template consists of three sections: a picture and a name, the details, and the goal of the persona, as Figure 19 shows. Unlike traditional persona descriptions, which are fully fledged, detail-rich user models, my template encourages you to start with simple, provisional personas that capture the essence of the character.

PICTURE & NAME	DETAILS	GOAL
What does the the persona look like? What is its name?	What are the persona's relevant characteristics and behaviors?	Why would the persona want to use or buy the product? What benefit should be achieved? Which problem should be solved?

FIGURE 19: A Persona Template

The section on the left of the template in Figure 19 captures the picture and the name of the persona. This makes it easier to develop empathy for the character and to refer to it. The latter comes in handy when you design the product and create scenarios, user stories, and other artifacts. I like to reuse the persona names in my user stories, for instance.

The middle section lists the relevant characteristics, attitudes, and behaviors of the persona. This can include demographics, job-related information, and hobbies. Don't make the mistake of listing everything that might be relevant, but focus on the details that are important in order to understand the persona. If a demographic attribute such as age or job role is not helpful, for example, then leave it out. Don't clutter your persona descriptions, and make sure that they are easy to understand. As a rule of thumb, your persona description should fit onto an A4 sheet of paper.

The section on the right states the problem that the persona wants to overcome, the benefit the character wants to gain, or the job it wants to get done. Make sure you describe the goal from the persona's perspective. Don't formulate it based on what you think your product should do, or what it can do today. Make the goal specific and state it clearly. While it's fine to list more than one problem or benefit, I recommend that you identify the main or primary reason for the persona to buy or use your product and state it at the top of the section. This creates focus and helps you make the right decisions.

When applying the persona template, start with the persona goal whenever you create something new, be it an adjacent or a disruptive product. Then consider the details and choose an appropriate name and picture. This avoids the risk of overlooking people who will benefit from your product, as I describe in more detail in the section "Segment the Market."

Find an Itch That's Worth Scratching

To create a successful product, you must understand why people would want to buy and use it. You must know which problem it solves, which pain or discomfort it removes, and which benefit or gain it provides. What's more, if the itch is not strong enough, your product is unlikely to be a success. Finding a problem that people want to have solved, or a benefit that people would no longer want to miss once they experienced it, is the most important step to achieving product success.

Let's look at the example of Sonos, a hi-fi system that consists of wireless speakers and audio components. It allows people to enjoy music by providing easy access to their digital music collection and to a range of streaming services from any device, while still offering a decent sound quality. It's simple and convenient to use. You no longer have to put a handheld device into a cradle or try to find a CD, switch on the amplifier, and look for the remote control. While the Sonos system does not solve a pressing issue, it is a product that is sticky. After starting to use it, I wouldn't want to miss it anymore.

Products like the Sonos hi-fi system are sometimes called *vitamins*, as they don't solve a pain or an urgent need. They rather provide a nice-to-have benefit, similar to vitamin supplements. Products that address a problem are referred to as *painkillers*. An Internet search engine like Bing or Google Search is a painkiller, as it solves the problem of finding information on the Internet. While the distinction between a vitamin and a painkiller is somewhat subjective, it shows that a product doesn't necessarily have to address a problem that people currently experience. Before I purchased the Sonos speakers, for instance, I wasn't aware of how cumbersome it is to listen to music using a traditional hi-fi system.

But no matter if it's a vitamin or a painkiller, your product must create a tangible benefit that is larger than the cost or hassle involved in obtaining and using the product. If the benefit is weak or the barrier to employing the product is high, then people are unlikely to buy and use your product. Let's take another look at Sonos. People who own traditional hi-fi components such as amplifiers and speakers are likely to find purchasing Sonos speakers unattractive, as this would render their stereo system obsolete. To address the issue, the company has created a product called Connect that allows individuals to reuse their existing hi-fi system while taking full advantage of Sonos's music-streaming capability. Connect creates a tangible benefit for music lovers—they can now stream music from any device to their stereo system—and it provides an additional revenue source for the company. You should therefore pay attention to any potential purchase and usage barriers and reduce or remove them, especially as you try to achieve product-market fit.

Clearly State the Value Your Product Creates

Once you have found a problem that your product should solve or a benefit it should provide, state it as clearly as you can. Avoid the mistake of working with a vague problem-benefit statement. Let's take two popular computer games, Gran Turismo and Minecraft.[24] The former is a car-racing game; the latter allows players to build three-dimensional structures out of cubes. At first glance, both products want to entertain

---

24   The choice of the Gran Turismo example is inspired by Elizalde (2014).

their users. People play the two games to have fun and feel a sense of achievement afterward. But the entertainment quality of the two games is very different. Gran Turismo allows its players to experience the thrill of racing. The players drive fast cars that look and behave much like their real-world counterparts. Minecraft, on the other hand, enables people to take joy in creating amazing structures, cities, and worlds, and sharing them with others.

To clearly state the value your product creates, describe what success looks like for the customers and users. In the case of a game like Gran Turismo, for example, you should explore what it means for the players to experience a great car-racing game. List the qualities that make up the desired experience, such as the thrill of driving fast cars that look and feel real. This will then allow you to design the right user experience and provide the right features, and it will help you market and sell the product effectively.

If you identify several problems that your product addresses or more than one benefit that it provides, then determine the primary one. Is the main benefit of a car-racing game, for instance, to experience the thrill of driving fast cars, or is it to beat other drivers? Identifying the primary benefit creates focus, and it makes it easier to test your assumptions and get the product right. I find that if I have a list with benefits or problems, and I am not able to determine the main one, I don't truly understand why people would want to use and buy the product.

Selecting the main problem or main benefit can require trading off user vs. customer needs; depending on your product, they may even be conflicting. For example, as a parent, I want my children to play computer games that are educational and nonviolent. But my kids have different ideas; they want games that they enjoy. Whenever I am faced with diverse customer and user needs, I tend to put the users first. I find that building a beneficial product—a product that does a great job for its users—is the basis for selling it successfully over an extended period of time.

Make Your Product Stand Out

Few products are groundbreaking innovations with no competition. Chances are that alternatives for your product exist. You should therefore ensure that your product stands out from the crowd and that people choose your product over competing offerings. This requires you to understand who your competitors are, what factors they compete on, and how your product scores against them.

The Strategy Canvas

A great tool to help you with this challenge is the Strategy Canvas, described in Kim and Mauborgne (2004) and shown in Figure 20.

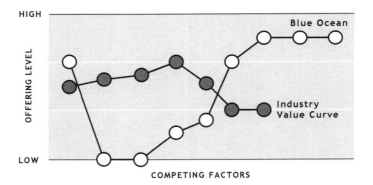

FIGURE 20: The Strategy Canvas

The horizontal axis of the Strategy Canvas captures the key factors your industry competes on. These factors include product, service, and delivery. The vertical axis describes the degree to which each competitor offers or invests in the factors. To apply the canvas, you first determine the key factors. These are the factors that products within the same category compete on, such as price, features, and design. Then evaluate to what degree your competitors fulfill these factors. This creates the industry value curve, represented by the dark line in Figure 20. You then assess your own product, which results in the white-dotted line in the diagram. The keys to applying the Strategy Canvas successfully are identifying the right factors and correctly evaluating the competition and your own product. Make sure you choose the factors that define the current standard in your market and are used to advertise and sell products, rather than the ones that favor your own product. Product reviews can help you discover the right factors, since they compare a product against the expected standard.

Once you have created your Strategy Canvas, compare the line of your product with the industry value curve. If the two are too close together, then you haven't differentiated your product sufficiently. You will subsequently find it hard to explain to your customers and users why they should choose your product. What you would like to see instead is a value curve that significantly diverges from the industry standard, like the white-dotted one in Figure 20. This is achieved by eliminating, reducing, and raising certain key factors, and by creating new ones. The area where your product does not face any competition is called a *blue market* or a *blue ocean* (the two last white dots). The Strategy Canvas therefore helps you not only determine where your competitors challenge one another; it also help you move into noncompetitive areas where growth opportunities exist.

Let's look at an example and use the canvas to compare the first iPhone to its competitors.

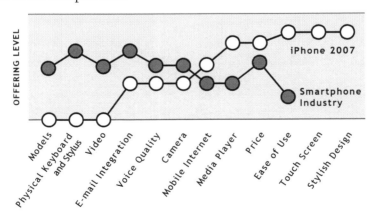

FIGURE 21: Strategy Canvas for the First iPhone[25]

---

25   The example is adapted from Islam and Ozcan (2012).

The Strategy Canvas in Figure 21 shows how the first iPhone ranked against its rivals, including the Nokia N95 and the BlackBerry Curve, using twelve factors ranging from stylish design to offering different models. When we compare the iPhone value curve to the industry standard, we see that Apple removed certain features, such as physical keyboard and video; reduced some, such as voice quality and e-mail integration; improved others, such as mobile Internet and media player; and created two new ones—a touch screen and a stylish design. By adding two new factors, Apple created a new *blue* market. If we fast-forward seven years and consider how the smartphone market has changed, we see that competitors have moved into the blue market and have matched the original iPhone's features. At the same time, Apple has created new factors and raised others, including the number and size of iPhone models, the battery life, and the camera and video capabilities.

The Kano Model

Another tool that helps you differentiate your product is the Kano model, first described in Kano (1984) and depicted in Figure 22.

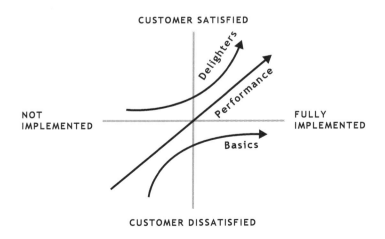

FIGURE 22: The Kano Model

The Kano model looks at two dimensions: the degree to which a feature is provided, shown on the horizontal axis, and the resulting customer satisfaction, depicted on the vertical axis. This allows us to distinguish different feature categories, including basics, performers, and delighters. Basic features are must-haves; without them you typically cannot sell your product. Making phone calls and sending text messages were basic features of the first iPhone, for instance. Performance features lead to a linear increase in satisfaction. They follow the principle "The more, the better." For example, mobile Internet and a media player were performers of the original iPhone. But performance features are not sufficient to differentiate your product in the marketplace. What you need are delighters. As the name suggests, these features delight or excite customers. The touch screen and the new stylish design were delighters of the first iPhone, for instance.

Comparing the Two Tools

If we compare the Strategy Canvas and the Kano model, then the delighters in the Kano model roughly correspond to the new factors of the Strategy Canvas, and the performers resemble the raised factors. What the Kano model lacks is an explicit reference to the competition and the notion of eliminating features. On the plus side, it recognizes that some features can be detractors and actually *prevent* people from using the product. For example, when Apple released the original iPhone, the company was concerned that users might not be able to operate the new device using the touch screen. The Kano model also predicts that delighters will become performers over time, and that performers will in turn into basics. In other words, the features that help differentiate and sell your product today won't ensure its attractiveness in the future. Take, for instance, the touch screen, one of the delighters of the first iPhone. Virtually all smartphones provide a touch screen today. The factor no longer makes a smartphone stand out. You therefore have to find ways to keep your product attractive and to prevent it from entering the decline stage—and from providing fewer and fewer benefits for your company.

Eliminate Features

When you compare a new product to the competition and determine what makes it special, it can be tempting to say: "Our product must provide all the competitors' features, but be better and offer more!" Similarly, as your product grows and matures, you may be tempted to add an increasing number of features to keep it competitive. Unfortunately, this can lead to an overly complex product that takes a lot of time and money to develop, has a vague value proposition, provides a poor user experience, and is expensive to maintain. The trick is not to blindly add features, but rather to explore which ones you can *remove*, thereby simplifying and decluttering your product.

A great tool for achieving this is the Eliminate-Reduce-Raise-Create grid (Kim and Mauborgne 2004). The grid encourages you to identify features that your product does not provide or that it offers to a lesser extent or in an inferior way compared with alternatives. It also helps you identify new and improved features. Let's build on the example from the previous section and apply the grid to the first iPhone.

ELIMINATE	RAISE
Physical keyboard and stylus, video, different models	Mobile Internet, digital music player, price
REDUCE	**CREATE**
Camera, voice quality, e-mail integration	Stylish design, touch screen

FIGURE 23: The Eliminate-Reduce-Raise-Create Grid

As Figure 23 shows, the first iPhone eliminated a number of smartphone features that were considered standards or must-haves when the product was launched in 2007. These included different models to choose from, a physical keyboard, and a stylus to write on the screen.[26] It also reduced a number of features, such as the voice, the camera quality, and the e-mail integration (no POP and no Exchange support). The iPhone also provided enhanced and genuinely new features. These included mobile Internet in the form of the Safari browser; the integration of the iPod with a mobile phone; a brand-new, eye-catching design; and a revolutionary touch screen. Removing and weakening features helped Apple reduce time to market; resulted in an uncluttered, easy-to-use product; and made the new and improved features stand out.

You can combine the Eliminate-Reduce-Raise-Create grid with the Strategy Canvas discussed in the last section and create a new, enhanced canvas, as Figure 24 shows.

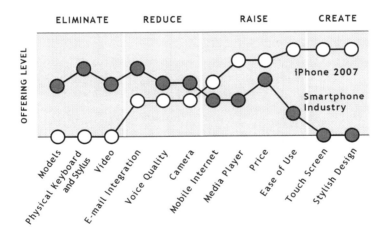

FIGURE 24: Strategy Canvas with Eliminate-Reduce-Raise-Create Grid

Eliminating the right features requires a solid understanding of your target group and the problem your product solves—as well as a good portion of courage. It's always easier to create a me-too product than to

---

26 With the release of the iPhone 5S and 5C, Apple deviated from its original one-model strategy.

create something different. As Steve Jobs once said: "Innovation is not about saying yes to everything. It's about saying no to all but the most crucial features."

Product Replacements

When you replace a product, it can be tempting to assume that all the features of the old product must be present in the new one. But this would be a mistake. Determine instead how large and heterogeneous the user group is, what job the product does for its users, and how it is actually employed. You can do this, for instance, by observing the users and reviewing the analytics data you have. Chances are that more than one feature made it into the product that does not create much value for the users. These features are prime candidates for elimination. If the user group is large and heterogeneous, then this provides an opportunity to unbundle the product or create product variants instead of continuing with one big product.

Offer a Great Customer Experience

Creating a product that addresses a problem or provides a tangible benefit for its customers and users is a big achievement. But even the best product will lead to dissatisfied customers if it is a hassle to evaluate, purchase, install, update, or uninstall it. People may consequently refrain from purchasing and using the product, particularly if they are not tech-loving innovators or visionary early adopters, but part of the mainstream market.[27] While this may sound trivial, I find it astounding how many companies focus so much on the features of their products that they forget about the context in which they are used. For example,

---

27 In his book *Crossing the Chasm*, Geoffrey Moore distinguishes five customer groups: innovators, early adopters, early majority, late majority, and laggards. The innovators are technology enthusiasts; they buy and use your product as soon as it is launched. The early adopters are visionaries who can see how the product benefits them. Together, they make up the early market, which corresponds to the introduction stage on the product life cycle model.

I recently decided to try out a new UK-based Internet television service that lets people watch movies and sports programs on demand without any subscription. I paid to watch a soccer game, only to discover when the game was about to start that my operating system was not compatible with the browser plug-in that the service used. While trying to resolve the issue, I ended up talking via a chat window to a customer service rep who unsympathetically told me there was nothing she could do. Frustrated, I asked for a refund. But instead of getting my money back, I received a bunch of marketing e-mails that explained me how great the company's services were.

As this example shows, it is important to get the overall customer experience of your product right and to remove any barriers that make it difficult for people to use the product. This is not only necessary to create satisfied customers and achieve sustained product success, it also allows you to differentiate your product from the competition. Here are three examples that show how this can be done: Sonos, for instance, has reduced the barrier to purchasing its wireless speakers by making it very simple to install the company's products and by providing a component that allows people to reuse their existing hi-fi equipment. Apple's retail stores make it enjoyable for people to discover, evaluate, and purchase Apple products; customers can also sign up for classes to learn how to better use those products. Amazon has improved the online shopping experience and has gained a competitive advantage by enabling customers to make purchases with a single click. These examples illustrate that you don't necessarily have to change the user-interface design or the features of your product to create more value. Getting the touch points right is equally powerful. This is particularly important to ready your product for the mainstream market and achieve growth. Innovators and early adopters may put up with a poor customer experience; but the early majority won't.

A great tool for capturing how people experience your product is the consumption map developed by MacMillan and McGrath (1997). The map captures the touch points customers and users have with your product and links them together in a chain, as Figure 25 illustrates.

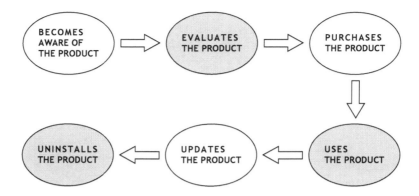

FIGURE 25: Sample Consumption Map

In order to create a consumption map for your product, follow the three steps below.[28] If your product serves several segments, then perform the exercise for each group.

1. First, determine how people currently interact with your product. Identify the key touch points, such as purchasing the product, installing it, and replacing it. Capture them as links in your chain. To get the chain right, observe how people employ the product, and analyze the usage data you have; this should result in a consumption map that represents the current state.

2. Analyze the customer experience at each link and determine how people interact with your product and your company. What prevents people from purchasing, using, or updating your product? Where do hiccups and problems occur? What happens, for example, when customers use your product on different devices? Is their experience seamless, or is it fragmented? Where do waiting and delays occur? How long does it take, for instance, until a support request is answered? How satisfied are people with the help they receive? How easy is

---

28 The steps are inspired by using value-stream mapping techniques. For more information, see Jones and Womack (2005).

it to return the product or cancel a subscription and receive a refund? Speak to the customer-service team to understand what the most common customer complaints are, then compare your product's consumption chain to the competition. Find out where your chain excels and where the competition is better.

3. Finally, create a new, enhanced consumption map. Investigate how you can add value and improve the customer experience at each link. Aim to provide what the customers want—where and when they want it—without wasting people's time or making it difficult for them. Explore how you can prevent errors and problems from occurring. How can you reduce waiting and delays? How can you make it easier and more convenient for people to evaluate, purchase, install, use, update, and uninstall your product? All touch points have to be right to create a truly great customer experience.

Carry out the steps above at least once at each product life cycle stage. This helps you identify short-term improvement measures; it also helps you prepare the product for the next life cycle stage and for the next set of customers with their specific expectations.

Build Variants and Unbundle Your Product

Creating product variants and unbundling your product are two powerful techniques that help you increase the benefits your product provides by launching a new, specialized version. A *product variant* is a variation or specialization of a product. Take, for instance, Microsoft's diagramming tool, Visio, which the company offers in three variants at the time of writing: Visio Standard, Visio Professional, and Visio Pro for Office 365.[29] Or take Strava, an app that I use to record and analyze my bicycle rides. Like many mobile apps, it comes in two variants: a basic

---

29 See: https://products.office.com/en-US/Visio/microsoft-visio-2013-plans-and-pricing-compare-visio-options.

one that is free, and a premium version that is not. Creating product variants establishes a *product line*, or a collection of related products, which is also called a *product family*. *Unbundling* your product means promoting a feature or feature set to a new product. A good example is Facebook Messenger, a software application that allows people to chat with their friends. The company took the messaging functionality originally included in its Facebook mobile app and released it as a stand-alone product in 2014. Another example is Foursquare's Swarm, described below.

Benefits

Unbundling features and introducing product variants can enable you to effectively grow the product, serve a new segment, generate more business benefits, and increase the product's competitiveness. Let's take a look at these benefits starting with achieving sustained growth. As a product grows and prospers, it often begins to serve an increasingly diverse market and it attracts more and more features. While this is a sign of success, it is also challenging to cater to the needs of an increasingly large and heterogeneous audience and to coordinate a growing number of development teams. It also carries the risk of offering a complex, feature-rich product plagued with a vague value proposition, a poor user experience, and high development cost. Creating new, specialized products simplifies your original offering, helps you avoid these issues, and lays the foundations for future growth. Let's look again at Facebook's Messenger app as an example. Unbundling the messaging feature from the main Facebook app streamlined the app, and it allowed the company to turn the Messenger app into a platform by adding new features, such as sending money to friends and communicating directly with businesses (Constine 2015).

Second, creating specialized products help you better serve an existing audience and take your product to a new target group. An example of the former is Foursquare's Swarm, a mobile app that used to be part of the main Foursquare app. The company discovered that the users of the Foursquare app hardly ever used the product to find places of interest, such as a specific type of restaurant, *and* to connect with their friends at the same time. It therefore unbundled the social interaction feature and released it as a new, standalone app called Swarm.[30] An example of a product that addressed a new target group is the iPod shuffle, a variant aimed at people who wanted a small, wearable iPod that could easily be taken on a run or bike ride.

Third, unbundling a product and introducing a new variant can increase the business benefits and open up new revenue streams. Microsoft charges a premium for the professional Visio variant compared to the standard version, for instance. Similarly, Strava Premium subscriptions are a major revenue source for the company, and Facebook Messenger, with features like sending money, generates a new revenue stream for the company and offers the opportunity to enter new markets.

Last but not least, both techniques can help you respond to market changes and increase your product's competitiveness. Google unbundled Google Drive into separate Docs, Sheets, and Slides apps to better compete against Apple's and Microsoft's productivity apps (D'Orazio 2014). Apple introduced larger smartphone variants in 2014—the iPhone 6 and 6 Plus—in response to the competition, including the Samsung Galaxy product line.

Drawbacks

Unfortunately, unbundling and creating variants don't come without drawbacks. One of them is the danger of offering too many specialized products, thus giving customers and users too much choice and potentially leaving them confused and frustrated. You should therefore ensure that you strike the right balance between having one big, monolithic

---

30 Foursquare Help Center, "Why are Foursquare and Swarm separate apps?" https://support.foursquare.com/hc/en-us/articles/202630254-Why-are-Foursquare-and-Swarm-separate-apps-.The example the company gave was that people often searched for the best fish tacos nearby, and they often searched to find where their friends were. But they almost never searched for places where their friends were that also offered great fish tacos.

product and offering too many specialized ones. Take Facebook as an example. While a stand-alone messaging app probably makes sense, breaking out more features from the main Facebook app into separate products could make it difficult for users to decide when to use each app, which would result in a poor user experience. Review and adjust your product lines regularly, and eliminate products when appropriate. Microsoft removed Visio Technical from its Visio product line in 2002, for example, and as mentioned earlier, Apple discontinued the iPod Classic in 2014, thereby streamlining the iPod product family.

A second drawback is that the newly created products may cannibalize your existing ones. Take the iPhone 6 Plus as an example. While the variant has helped Apple fend off competition from other smartphone manufacturers, the product seems to have cannibalized another Apple product, the iPad Mini (Preece 2015). Similarly, releasing Facebook Messenger as a separate product that no longer needs a Facebook account may attract new users, but it may also result in some people no longer using the main Facebook app.

Third, introducing a product family creates the need for portfolio management. Dependencies of the family members have to be managed, and the release dates have to be coordinated. Take Microsoft Office as an example. New versions of the Office products are released at the same time. (For more information on portfolio management, please refer to Part 2.)

Shared Assets and Platforms

When you spin off a feature or develop a new variant, you should consider creating standards and assets—including components, services, and other architectural building blocks—that the product family members share. This ensures a consistent user experience across the different products, and it can reduce the development effort required. It would be undesirable if the Google Docs, Sheets, and Slides apps followed different user-interaction and user-design principles, for instance. People would find it difficult to switch between the apps, which might affect engagement and market share. Similarly, if the teams developing the different apps all created their own user-interface layers, there would be considerable code duplication and added development costs.

Once you have created a set of shared assets, you may choose to group them into a platform, as shown in Figure 26. Note that a platform can provide shared front-end assets, such as a graphical user interface (GUI) library, as well as back-end resources, like a data-access layer.

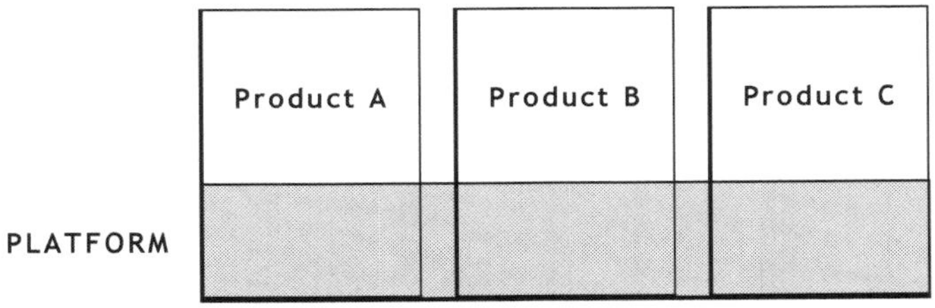

FIGURE 26: Platform as a Collection of Shared Assets

One example of a successful platform is Siemens Healthcare's medical-imaging software *syngo*. The platform standardizes how images are read, stored, and shared across a range of Siemens Healthcare products, including MRI and CT scanners. This makes it easier for the hospital staff to work with different syngo-based products, and it reduces the development time and cost for Siemens.[31]

Breaking out a feature or creating a variant is often not a trial task, and it can require some major development work, depending on how modular the architecture is. The same is true for creating shared assets and a platform. I therefore recommend that you explicitly plan the necessary work and capture it on your product roadmap, as described in more detail in Part 2.

---

31 See http://www.healthcare.siemens.com/medical-imaging-it for more information.

Summary

Table 5 summarizes the benefits and drawbacks of the two techniques.

TABLE 5: Benefits and Drawbacks of Unbundling vs.
Creating Variants

Benefits	Drawbacks
• Makes it easier to grow the product and add new features; improves the user experience by simplifying the product.	• Customers and users may be given too much choice, leaving them feeling confused or overwhelmed.
• Enables you to take the product to a new market or segment or to address the needs of a specific group.	• Existing products may be cannibalized.
• Helps you generate more business benefits; creates an opportunity to evolve the business model and open up new revenue streams.	• Portfolio management is required to coordinate the members of the product family.
• Can increase the product's competitiveness and help you respond to market changes.	• Shared assets, and possibly a platform, have to be developed.

Create a Product Bundle

The opposite of unbundling a product is combining separate products into a *bundle*: a newly formed, bigger offering. For example, Microsoft Office is a software bundle that includes Word, Excel, and PowerPoint. You can't license or subscribe to Word individually—only in combination with other Office products. As always, there are benefits and drawbacks to this strategy.

Benefits

Creating a product bundle is helpful when the individual products are too small or not attractive enough to succeed on their own. Mobile operating systems, like Windows Phone and iOS, come with preinstalled apps, for instance, to make the platforms more appealing. Bundling is also a strategy to increase sales—think of McDonald's Happy Meal, which gives you a hamburger, French fries, and a drink for less than buying the items individually. The idea is that customers spend more money and buy more products if they receive a bundle discount. Finally, bundling can help you gain an advantage over the competition. Combining Internet Explorer and Windows helped Microsoft win the first "browser war" in the late 1990s, for example.[32]

Drawbacks

While bundling can be helpful, you should avoid the following three mistakes. First, don't turn people off by creating bundles that are too big. When Netscape came under pressure in the first browser war, the company tried to make its product more attractive and defend its market share by adding several products to its browser, including an e-mail client and a news client. The resulting bundle was called the Netscape Communicator. Unfortunately, it was rather bloated and complex, which added to Netscape's worries rather than alleviating them. I still remember changing from the Navigator to the Communicator and finding the new product slow and complicated to use.

Second, don't restrict the buying choices of your customers too much. Take Microsoft Office as an example. I would love to subscribe to the latest Word version, but having to pay for a bundle that contains products for which have no use, prevents me from doing so. If that's the case for a larger group of people, then the bundling strategy might be disadvantageous for Microsoft, given that the product suite is a major revenue source for the company.[33]

Finally, don't forget to harmonize the user experience across the bundle to make it easy for users to change between products. As you would expect, the key functions such as opening and saving document work in the same way, have the same visual representation, and are found in the same place for the various Office products, for instance. Identify the necessary user experience work, such as creating shared

---

32   The company used the popularity of its operating system to significantly increase its browser market share and to defeat Netscape Navigator. For more information, see http://en.wikipedia.org/wiki/Browser_wars.

33   Before Microsoft released Word as part of Office for Windows in 1990, it was available as a stand-alone product for MS-DOS. See https://en.wikipedia.org/wiki/Microsoft_Word.

user-interaction and user-interface design standards, and capture it on your product roadmap.

(Re-) Position Your Product

Creating a successful product requires more than simply delivering the right features. It also involves developing a strong brand that clearly communicates what your product stands for and that resonates with its customers and users. Take brands like Apple, Google, Amazon, Facebook, and Microsoft—they all give rise to different associations and feelings. The same is true for strong product brands such as iPhone, Google Search, Amazon Marketplace, Facebook Messenger, and Word. The value of a brand is the power to capture customer loyalty and preference. Customers buy products not only because they do a good job for them, but also because the customers connect with the brand. Product strategy and brand should therefore be closely aligned.

In order to build a strong product brand, be clear on your company's overall branding strategy and decide if and how to create a subbrand for your product. Google, for example, combines the Google main brand with product-specific subbrands, resulting in product names like Google Search and Google Maps. Great brand names are authentic and represent the product they stand for; they create a positive emotional response with the customers, and they are concise and simple enough to become a part of the customers' vocabulary and synonymous with the items they represent. Take, for example, how the verb *to google* has come to mean "search for information on the Internet."

If you create a product that users and customers don't associate with the company brand, then it may be best to create a new brand. Examples include Lexus, which has allowed Toyota to sell luxury cars, and Smart, which has enabled Daimler to sell compact city cars. It would have probably been a mistake to try to sell luxury cars under the Toyota name or city cars under the Mercedes-Benz brand.

If you want to take your product to a new market or extend its life cycle, you should consider repositioning or rebranding it. Microsoft, for instance, implemented a gradual rebranding of its product range in 2011 and 2012. This included redesigning its logos and updating the look and feel of its products, using the principles and concepts of the Metro design language (Howard 2013). Microsoft's goal was to change the perception of its brands and products and to make them look fresh and attractive again. In the same time frame, Microsoft released a series of updated products, including Windows 8 and Windows Phone 8, as well as new products, such as Surface, a tablet computer designed and manufactured by the company.

STRATEGY VALIDATION

Whenever you create a new product or make a bigger change to an existing one, such as unbundling it or taking it to a new market, your strategy is likely to contain risks. For example, the need for your product might not be strong enough, the segment you've chosen might not be right, or the technologies might not be feasible. In order to maximize the chances of releasing a successful product, you should systematically identify and address the key risks before you fully implement the new strategy.

Iteratively Test and Correct Your Strategy

A great way to validate the product strategy is to follow an iterative approach along the lines suggested in the book *The Lean Startup* (Ries 2011). Start by selecting the biggest risk: the uncertainty that must be addressed now so that you don't take the product in the wrong direction and experience late failure—that is, figuring out at a late stage that you are building a product that nobody really wants or needs. Next, determine how you can best address the risk—for instance, by observing target users, interviewing customers, or employing a minimum viable product (MVP). Carry out the necessary work and collect the relevant feedback or data. Then analyze the results and use the newly gained insights to decide if you should pivot, persevere, or stop—if you should stick with your strategy, change it, or no longer pursue your vision—and take the appropriate actions accordingly. Follow this process until no crucial risks are left, you are confident that your strategy is correct, and you have enough evidence to support it—or until you have run out of time and money. Figure 27 illustrates this process.

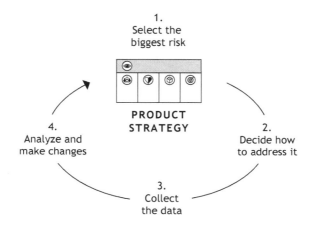

FIGURE 27: Testing the Product Strategy

Iteratively reworking the product strategy encourages you to carry out just enough market research just in time to avoid too much or too little research. It also suggests a risk-driven approach—addressing the biggest risks first so that you can quickly understand which parts of your strategy are working and which are not, thus avoiding late failure. As you iterate your strategy, you should see its uncertainty decrease; fewer and fewer risks should be present, and the contents should become clearer and more refined, as Figure 28 illustrates.

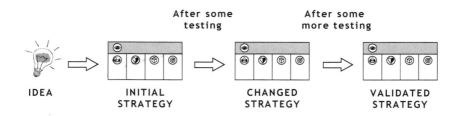

FIGURE 28: The Strategy Changes

Determine the Necessary Validation Effort

How much validation is required depends on the innovation strategy you follow. Core innovations carry few risks and unknowns, and the validation effort is low: typically ranging from zero effort to a few hours or days. Adjacent innovations exhibit a much higher level of risk and require a medium validation effort; you may have to spend several weeks addressing the key risks in your product strategy. Disruptive products are even riskier than adjacent ones. As a result, they require a high validation effort, and it may take you several months to develop a valid strategy. Figure 29 illustrates the correlation between innovation type and validation effort by using the Innovation Ambition Matrix discussed earlier.

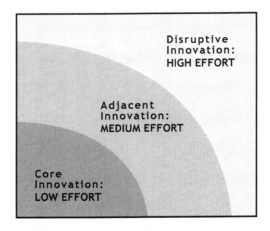

FIGURE 29: Determining the Validation Effort

Note that the figures above are only rough guidelines. You may find that the actual validation effort for your product is higher or lower than stated. Take the story in Jeffrey Liker's (2004) book *The Toyota Way*, about Toyota's chief engineer spending a year in California living the life and driving BMWs, Mercedes-Benzes, and other luxury cars in order to thoroughly understand the target market before building the very first Lexus car. As Toyota entered an existing market with a new product (adjacent innovation), it had to create a product that could compete with the offerings of the established luxury-car brands. Investing enough time to thoroughly understand the market was thus the right choice.

Involve the Right People

Getting the product strategy right is a team sport, particularly for adjacent and disruptive products. As the person in charge of the product, identifying and addressing all the risks and making the right decisions on your own is likely to be overwhelming. You will therefore benefit from the support of the stakeholders. As discussed earlier, these include members of the development team and representatives from other business groups, such as marketing, sales, support, legal, and finance, as well as a ScrumMaster or coach.

The development-team members should consist of a user experience (UX) designer, a programmer, and a tester. Their job is to help you assess the technical feasibility of the product, identify and address technical risks, and build prototypes. The business-group members share their perspectives, knowledge, and ideas and help you identify and address risks related to marketing, selling, and supporting the product. A sales rep, for instance, may be able to get you in touch with target customers and users; a UX designer may carry out research work, such as directly observing users, together with you; and a developer and tester may evaluate different technology and architecture options for you. The ScrumMaster facilitates collaboration and advises on process issues—for example, how to best use a Kanban board to visualize and track the validation work. Together they make up the *players*: the key stakeholders who have an interest in your product and the power to influence it, as I discuss in the section "Engage the Stakeholders."

How closely you should collaborate with the stakeholders, and how much they should participate in the validation work depends on the amount of uncertainty present. If you work on a disruptive product or on a new adjacent one, then I recommend that you opt for close collaboration and form a team similar to the one shown in Figure 30. This team is also called *the product discovery team*.[34] Otherwise, a looser, on-demand collaboration may be sufficient.

FIGURE 30: The Product Discovery Team

In order to have an effective product discovery team in place, ensure that the necessary skills are present, that the team is stable, that its members can dedicate enough time to the validation work, and that they are collocated. If you lack the necessary skills, then the quality and speed of the work will suffer. If the team is not stable and its composition changes, you will experience handoffs, loss of knowledge, and delays. While people don't necessarily have to be full-time members, progress will be slow if the team members don't have enough availability. And if the team is not collocated, collaboration is less effective. When in doubt, weigh a potential delay against an increase in cost—

---

34 Cagan (2011) coined the term *product discovery team*. He originally used it to refer to the product manager, the lead user experience designer, and the lead developer. Ries (2009) calls the product discovery team *problem team*, since the team validates that a problem exists that is worthwhile to address.

for example, the cost to collocate the individuals or to free them from other tasks. A great way to bring the right people together is to form an incubator, a technique I discuss in the section "Turn Failure into Opportunity."

Collaborating with the key stakeholders, or players, provides you with a number of benefits. It encourages shared ownership, builds strong buy-in, leverages the creativity of the entire group, results in better decisions, and mitigates *cognitive biases*, which are faults in our thinking that cause us to draw the wrong conclusions, including overlooking or misinterpreting valuable information. As mentioned before, don't forget that collaboration requires leadership. As the person in charge of the product, you should lead the strategy-validation work. Don't shy away from difficult conversations, have the courage to make a decision if people can't agree, and use data to test ideas and back up decisions, as I describe in the next section.

Use Data to Make Decisions

The process of capturing and subsequently testing and changing the product strategy is built on the idea that collecting feedback, data, and empirical evidence is necessary to make the right decisions. This is not to say that intuition and gut feeling are unimportant—they are great for coming up with ideas and new options. But if you make decisions only on the basis of what you believe, then you risk making poor decisions; after all, your belief may well be wrong. This does not only happen at work, as the following example shows. I enjoy riding my bicycle, and as mentioned before, I use Strava to record my rides. When I compare the data Strava collects to my riding experience, it sometimes turns out that my perception is wrong—that I was not as fast as I thought, for instance, even though I tried hard. If I blindly trusted my gut feeling, then this would be a poor basis for improving my performance and becoming a better cyclist. Another drawback of making decisions purely based on intuition, opinions, and beliefs is that in the case of conflict, the person with the bigger clout, the more authority, and the greater influence often wins. To put it differently, with the right data you have a chance to successfully argue against the opinion and views of powerful stakeholders; without data, it may be difficult, and the *HiPPO*—the highest-paid person's opinion—may win.

But be aware that as human beings, we all have cognitive biases that can cause us to collect the wrong data or to misinterpret it. Confirmation bias, for instance, is the tendency to favor information that confirms our preconceptions, while self-serving bias is the tendency to claim more responsibility for our successes than our failures. You can't easily escape these biases, but you can mitigate them by collecting and analyzing the data together with other people, as this tends to balance out individual preferences, beliefs, and preconceptions.

Turn Failure into Opportunity

Established businesses often optimize their processes, tools, and organizations for core innovations in order to improve existing products for existing customers. Core innovations require a focus on operational excellence and efficiency. While failures and mistakes are likely to have a negative impact on the business performance and are thus discouraged, disruptive and adjacent products exhibit a high degree of uncertainty and risk. This necessitates learning and experimentation, which in turn creates the need for making mistakes. As Albert Einstein famously said, "A person who never made a mistake never tried anything new." Making mistakes and failing are valuable, of course, only if they enable us to learn, to discover a new idea, or to learn that an idea or assumption is wrong. Thomas Edison, the founder of GE and the creator of the first commercially successful electric light bulb, no doubt knew about the need to fail when he said: "If I find 10,000 ways something won't work, I haven't failed. I am not discouraged, because every wrong attempt discarded is another step forward." If failure teaches you something useful, then it truly is a step toward success.

Because making mistakes and experiencing failure are unavoidable when we create something new, you should expect to fail and to receive feedback and data that shows your strategy is at least partially incorrect. If you never fail, if you always receive positive feedback, you should stop and reflect. Chances are that you are not addressing the right risks, that your test group and/or methods are wrong, or that you are misinterpreting the data. As mentioned earlier, watch out for the common bias of confirming your own ideas, as mentioned earlier. Challenge yourself; look for issues and weaknesses; try to intentionally invalidate your ideas. When you carry out a product demo or solution interview, explicitly ask the interviewees, for example, what is wrong or not quite right with the product, and ask how the customer experience could be further improved. If you don't get any negative feedback, if your ideas are never invalidated, then you won't learn enough.

To enable fast failure and learning, you may have to create a fail-safe environment where it is acceptable to make mistakes, particularly if you work for a company that is focused on core innovations. A great way to establish such an environment is the use of an incubator. An incubator is a new, temporary business unit that is loosely coupled to the rest of the organization. It offers the necessary autonomy to innovate—and to fail—fast. As Peter Drucker writes in his book *Innovation and Entrepreneurship*, "The best, and perhaps the only, way to avoid killing off the new...is to set up the innovative project from the start as a separate business" (1985, 163).

An incubator is particularly valuable for disruptive products due to the high amount of uncertainty and risk such products exhibit.[35] But incubators also benefit adjacent innovations, as the following example shows. The first Scrum project I worked on back in 2004 was tasked with creating a new digital telecommunications product, which is now a part of the OpenScape Unified Communications

---

35   Christensen and Raynor (2013) argue in Part 4 of their book that an incubator is mandatory for succeeding with disruptive innovations.

suite. The development effort took place at Siemens, a company that is over a hundred years old and has more than four hundred thousand employees. In order to create an incubator, we hired new offices and collocated people from different parts of the company. This gave the team the ability to collaborate effectively and provided them with the freedom to think outside the box, to try new things, to fail, and to learn fast. Had the team members been embedded in their respective organizations, it would have been impossible to achieve the same success.

There are, of course, alternatives to using an incubator. An example is Google's 20-percent rule. Engineers can spend up to 20 percent of their time exploring new ideas, an approach that helped create the Google Chrome browser, for instance. Another alternative is a company-internal hackathon, where people come together for one or more days to try out new ideas. Facebook's *Like* button was conceived in a hackathon, for example.[36] Whichever approach you choose, ensure that you create an environment that allows you to fail and to learn fast when working on adjacent and disruptive products.

While failure is unavoidable when creating something new, it is most helpful to fail early on. The earlier you fail, the cheaper the failure tends to be. The impact is less severe, and you will have more options to take corrective actions. The later you fail, the harder it becomes. The consequences for your product and your organization are more severe. You may also find accepting failure more difficult, as you may have become attached to your ideas.

Get Out of the Building

Whatever you do to test your product strategy, follow Steve Blank's (2014) advice and "get out of the building." Visit your target customers and users to understand their needs and to see the environment where your product will be used—for example, on the train, in a supermarket,

---

36   Source: http://en.wikipedia.org/wiki/Hackathon, retrieved on January 19, 2015.

at people's homes, or at their workplaces. "Go out to look, to ask, to listen," as Drucker (1985, 135) puts it. You won't discover the truth in your office.

Make sure you directly interact with the customers and the users and study the market yourself. Don't solely rely on what others tell you about the market and the product; don't blindly trust the sales group, support, management, or a market research company, as the following example shows. A client of mine, a large media company, spent a lot of time and money on developing a beautiful, powerful app. After its launch, the company discovered that users only employed a small subset of the features. What went wrong? The company had hired an agency to carry out the user research work and validate the strategy. For whatever reason—be it fear of failure or an insufficient understanding of the product's value proposition—the agency reported back that all the feedback on early prototypes was positive and that the strategy was just right.

"Get out of the building" is not only applicable for brand-new products. You should also follow it for an existing product, even if you have plenty of analytics data available. There is a real difference between analyzing data and observing people as they interact with your product. I like to suggest that product managers visit customers and users at least once per quarter. This ensures that you regularly meet, observe, and talk to the people who should benefit from your product. When interacting with customers and users, keep an open mind. Be willing to observe, listen, and learn. . Don't be put off by the effort required to contact people. Recruiting a test group can be as easy as sending out a targeted tweet or e-mail. The reward might be a great idea for how to improve your product.

Identify the Biggest Risk

Testing your product strategy requires that you identify the biggest risk or leap-of-faith assumption. To do this, determine the statements in your strategy that are uncertain and that could cause damage and have a negative impact on the product's success. A successful product has to address the right market and the right needs, provide the right features and use the right technologies, and deliver the right business goals, as Figure 31 illustrates. You should therefore look for risks that affect the market and the needs, the features and the technologies, and the business goals of your product.

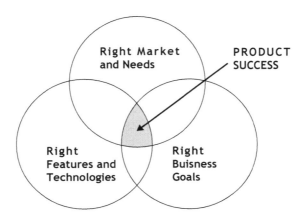

FIGURE 31: The Product Success Conditions[37]

Don't make the mistake of being primarily concerned with technical feasibility. No matter how technologically advanced your product is, if it does not create enough value for its customers and users, it is unlikely to be a success. Instead, tackle the risks related to the market and the needs first. If there is no market for your product, or if the product's value proposition is weak, then coming up with cool features or amazing technologies is not going to help you. Table 6 provides several sample questions to help you discover the major risks contained in your strategy. Use them as a starting point, discard questions that are irrelevant, and add additional ones that might be missing.

---

37   The diagram is based on the design constraints in Brown (2009, 15).

TABLE 6: Risks and Sample Questions

Risks	Sample Questions
Market and Needs	Will removing the problem you want to solve make a real difference to the customers and users? Is the benefit the product creates something people would not want to miss once they have experienced it? Are you confident that you have selected the right market segment, and that you are addressing the right people? Is the target group clear-cut? Are you able to tell who is in your target group and who is not? Do you have a rough idea of how big the market is? Are there any major market entry barriers?
Features and Technologies	Will the product be able to do a great job for the users and customers? Can you list the top three features that will make people want to use or buy the product? Does the product offer a clear and compelling advantage over the competitors' products? Are you clear on the branding strategy? What are the key characteristics of the desired user experience? Is it feasible to develop the product? Are the technologies required available? Are they mature enough? Does your organization have the necessary skills to use them effectively? Are enough people with the right skills available, and if not, can you recruit them?
Business Goals	Are you confident that it's worthwhile to develop, market, sell, and support the product? Are you clear on the business goals the product should deliver? Can you quantify and measure the desired business benefits? Do you know which one is your number one goal? Do you understand how the goals can be achieved? What business model will you use? Are you confident that the business model will work?

As mentioned previously, once you have identified the risks contained in your strategy, choose the most crucial one—the risk that must be addressed now to avoid making the wrong decisions and experiencing late failure. As a rule of thumb, work on one risk at a time. This creates focus and facilitates collaboration, and it makes it easier to collect and analyze the relevant data.

A simple yet effective way to determine the most important risk is to play the Red Dot Game.[38] Here is how it works. After visualizing your product strategy—for instance, by printing it out and putting it up on the office wall—give three adhesive red dots to everybody involved in validating the product strategy. Ask the players to put the dots next to the statements they are most unsure or concerned about. Then count

---

38   Smith and Pichler (2005) described an early version of this game.

the points per statement. If there is a clear winner, briefly discuss the risk, along with the damage it can cause. If not, carry out another round among those risks that have the most dots. Stop voting when you reach consensus. This game takes advantage of the collective wisdom of the team and uses the team members' perceptions to determine the risks and their severity rather than trying to quantify the impact and probability of each risk. It is fast and usually good enough.

Finally, ask yourself how you will be able to tell that you have successfully resolved the risk. Say I decided to conduct problem interviews (discussed below) to mitigate the danger of selecting the wrong segment for my healthy-eating app. How can I then tell if I succeeded in choosing the right group? How many people should I interview? How many of those have to experience unhealthy eating as an issue? It is therefore important that you consider the success criteria for addressing the risk up front. Without clear criteria in place, you may not able to correctly analyze the data you gather, and you may draw the wrong decision.

Choose the Right Validation Techniques

Once you have determined the biggest risk, you need to decide how to best address it. In other words, tackling the risk becomes your goal. This involves two things. First, select the right validation technique—the method that allows you to address the risk and to reduce the uncertainty. Second, choose the right test group—the people who should provide relevant feedback or data. Sample validation techniques include observing users, interviewing customers, creating a minimum viable product (MVP), and developing a *spike*, which I describe in more detail in the next sections.

Don't make the mistake of relying on a single method, particularly not over an extended time. Every validation technique has its strengths and weaknesses; none is perfect. Select the technique that is best suited to address your risk. As a rule of thumb, use qualitative methods, such as directly observing people, together with quantitative ones, for example, releasing an MVP. The benefit of qualitative techniques is that you interact directly with the customers and users. This helps you understand *why* people behave in a certain way. The benefit of quantitative methods is that you can connect with a larger group. This reduces the risk of collecting non-representative data and making the wrong decisions. If several techniques are equally well suited for tackling a risk, then choose the quickest and cheapest one. If you could use a paper-based prototype or an executable, software-based one, for instance, then opt for the former, as it is likely to be quicker and cheaper to build.

Whichever techniques you choose, separate data analysis from data collection. Avoid drawing any conclusions while you are still gathering the relevant information, as this can influence your data-collection work and cause you to make the wrong decisions. Wait with the analysis until enough data becomes available.

Directly Observe Customers and Users

Direct observation means carefully watching how the target customers and users carry out a job. It helps you validate that you have picked the right target group and that its members are likely to benefit from your product. Using my healthy-eating app as an example, let's assume that I have chosen young, male professionals as my target group. In order to learn more about them and to understand if they would benefit from the product, I could study their eating behavior and observe them buying and eating food during their lunch break, whether it is in a canteen, a restaurant, or a public space.

Observation is a powerful technique not only for developing a new product, but also for spotting opportunities to improve an existing one—even if you employ an analytics tool and have plenty of usage data available. Watching people brings a new dimension to understanding how they use your product, and why they may be struggling with some features or not employing them at all. Therefore, get out of the office and study your users in the wild. If that's not possible, then ask selected members of your target group if you can watch them remotely, via Skype screen sharing, for example, to see how they carry out the relevant tasks.

As you carry out direct observation, focus on your research goal and the risk you want to address, and be patient, nonintrusive, and open-minded. Being patient and gentle mitigates the risk that people will act differently with someone watching them (this is known as the *observer effect*). Having an open mind and observing without preconceived notions will help you see clearly; it reduces the risk that your cognitive biases distort what you see.

Carry Out Problem Interviews

Problem interviews are structured conversations with target users and customers. The goal is to find out how they currently carry out the relevant activities, what works well for them, and what does not. Problem interviews help you discover whether you have selected the right target group and a problem that's worth solving. Say that I am still working on my healthy-eating app, and I am not sure if healthy eating is an issue for young male professionals. I could then schedule one-on-one interviews with members of the target group and ask them what, when, and how much they eat; if the food they consume and the way they eat contributes to their wellbeing; if they are aware of what and how much they eat; if they purposefully choose their food; if they are happy with their weight; if they exercise regularly; and if fitness and health are important to them.

To conduct effective problem interviews, be clear on the risk you need to address and prepare for the conversations. Carefully select the questions and record the answers. Be friendly and open. Be careful not to mention your product—discovering the right user interface and interaction design and finding the right features is not the objective at this stage. Don't ask leading questions that encourage people to provide a certain answer, for instance, "You are concerned about eating healthily and really want to do something about it, don't you?" This puts the interviewee in a corner and tempts the individual to say yes just to please you. Be careful not to comment on the answers, whether in verbal or in nonverbal form—for example, by raising your eyebrows or by sighing. Ask clarifying questions if you cannot fully understand the answer. Don't forget to ask for basic demographic information, such as name, age, and job. Make sure your interviews last no more than fifteen minutes to find enough people who are willing to be interviewed. Consider offering a small incentive or thank-you token such as a voucher. As with observing people, I recommend conducting between five and ten problem interviews to address any given risk.

Create Minimum Viable Products

A minimum viable product (MVP) is an initial product version that allows you to learn how people actually use your product, even though it is still very limited and may only vaguely represent the product it will eventually become (Ries 2009). MVPs are powerful because they build on a fundamental insight—we can't know for sure if a product or a feature creates value for the customers until people start using it. The earlier we provide something that resembles the product to the users, the sooner we can test our ideas and the quicker we learn if we are building the right thing.

MVPs come in different shapes and sizes, depending on their purpose. For instance, I used *workshops* and *blog posts* as MVPs to test whether there was demand for a product strategy and roadmapping book such as this, which aspects of these topics people commonly struggle with, and whether I would be able to provide helpful advice. Other sample MVPs include *videos*, which Dropbox used to test its original product idea; *landing pages*, where people are directed after clicking a link from an ad, e-mail, or other campaign; *product* or *feature fakes*, which are also called *Wizard of Oz* MVPs; and *concierge* MVPs, where the products or services are manually provided. An example of the latter is to go shopping for selected customers instead of building an online shopping experience. Choose the MVP that allows you to test your assumption or risk in the quickest and cheapest way possible.

MVPs can help you understand if there is sufficient demand for your product, if its exciters really excite the users, if your ideas about the user experience are correct, if the marketing and sales channels work, or if the product is priced correctly. For example, I might be tempted to choose a freemium model for my healthy-eating app. Using this model, I would give away a basic version for free and aim to generate revenue through in-app purchases. While this model is rather popular, it carries a significant risk: people may be so happy with the basic version that they don't make any in-app purchases. At the same time, if the basic version is too thin, the app is unlikely to attract enough users, which will then make it difficult to generate the desired revenue. In order to address the risk, I could develop an initial pricing model and use a product or feature fake to find out if people would be willing to pay a specific amount for the product or functionality.

Build Spikes to Assess Technical Feasibility

A spike is a throwaway prototype that addresses a specific technology or architecture risk. It helps you discover if you can develop the product, and how much effort it is likely to require. That's important, as the best product idea is useless if you don't have the people with the right skills to build the product, if the technologies required don't exist or aren't mature enough, or the product is simply unaffordable to build. For instance, a spike could help me evaluate what it takes to develop my healthy-eating product as an iOS app and allow me to explore core technologies such as Objective-C, Xcode, Cocoa, and UIKit.

Employing spikes also provides the opportunity to start thinking about the development and test environments, and to investigate any third-party software that may be part of the product. This helps the development team prep for the first sprint, and it gives you a rough understanding of the licensing cost, which may affect your business goals and your business model.

While spikes can be very helpful, avoid the trap of creating a big up-front design for your product. Only tackle the key risks, and don't worry about the detailed technical design. You want to be confident that you can build the product in a reasonable time frame and on a realistic budget, but you don't want to make all architecture decisions up front. The detailed technical design should evolve during the development of the product (assuming that uncertainty and change are present).

Pivot, Persevere, or Stop

Once you have collected the relevant feedback or data, review and analyze it. Ask yourself if your overall strategy is valid. Your initial product strategy may contain plenty of assumptions and risks, and you may well discover that the strategy is *wrong* and does not work. If that's the case, then you have two choices: stop and let go of your vision, or stick with the vision and change the strategy, which is also called a *pivot*. If your strategy does work, then you should leverage the new insights to adjust and improve it. In other words, you persevere. Figure 32 illustrates this approach.

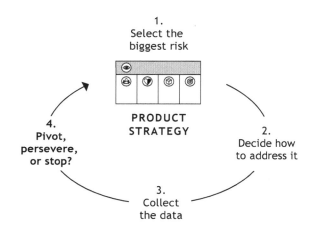

FIGURE 32: Pivot, Persevere, or Stop?

To illustrate what pivoting means, let's take my healthy-eating app as an example. If I cannot find a large enough group that would benefit from using a digital product to improve their eating habits, I could decide to pivot and employ a new strategy instead. This might be writing a book, running workshops, or creating an e-learning tutorial. The new strategy would result in a fundamentally different product. But it would still help me realize my vision.

Pivoting is attractive only if you pivot early, when the cost of changing direction is comparatively low. You should therefore aim to find out quickly if anything is wrong with your strategy, and if you need to fail, then fail fast. While a late pivot can happen, you should avoid it, because the later it occurs, the more difficult and costly it is likely to be. And if you pivot repeatedly, you should stop and reflect: chances are that you are not moving toward an attainable vision, but rather chasing an ever-changing dream.

Use Agile Techniques to Manage the Validation Work

This section describes three agile techniques for managing the validation work: timeboxing the validation activities; using a Kanban board to visualize, organize, and track the work; and conducting regular review meetings.

Timebox the Work

Allocating enough time and money to validate the product strategy can be tricky. Knowing the innovation type of your product is not enough to anticipate all the key risks and estimate the effort necessary to address them; new risks often emerge as part of the validation work. Luckily, there is a straightforward solution: timebox your strategy work. A time box is a fixed period of time, such as four weeks, that cannot be extended. At the end of the time box, the work stops, and you reflect on what has been achieved so far. If the work has not been completed and your strategy still contains significant risks, you have two options: add another time box—and possibly pivot—or stop the work. Figure 33 illustrates the idea of timeboxing the validation work.

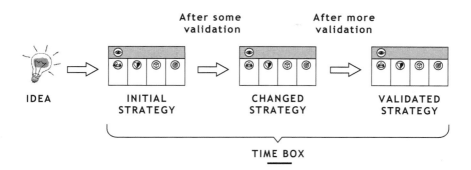

FIGURE 33: Timeboxed Strategy Work

I recommend that you work with time boxes that are no longer than four weeks, even if you're working on adjacent or disruptive innovations. Shorter time boxes create focus and make the progress of the validation work more transparent than longer ones. You can think of the time box as a strategy sprint: a cycle with objective to test and develop the product strategy.[39]

Use a Kanban Board

Once you have determined the work necessary to validate your initial product strategy, you should manage and track it. An excellent way to do this is by capturing the relevant tasks on a simple Kanban board, as pictured in Figure 34.[40]

---

39 Ash Maurya has suggested a similar concept called the Lean Sprint: http://ash-maurya.com/the-lean-sprint/. Because technically speaking, sprints are time-boxed and protected iterations that create product increments, I don't use the term *sprint* to refer to time boxes or cycles that carry out strategy work.

40 For more information on Kanban and working with a Kanban board, refer to Anderson (2010).

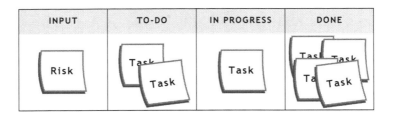

FIGURE 34: A Simple Kanban Board for Strategy Testing

To illustrate how you can work with the Kanban board above, let's assume I want to address the risk of selecting the wrong target group for my healthy-eating app. I would capture the risk on a paper card and add it to the "Input" column. Next I would identify the tasks necessary to address the risk, such as carrying out direct observation and interviewing people and analyzing the data. I would then add the tasks to the "To-Do" column. When I start working on a task, I move it to the "In Progress" column, and after completing the task, I move the card to the "Done" column. If you want to work on two risks in parallel, then simply add a new risk card with the necessary tasks below the first risk. But remember that working on multiple risks can make it more difficult to collect the right data and to analyze it correctly.

Working with a Kanban board visualizes the work to be done and the progress made, facilitates collaboration, and encourages ownership and self-organization. That's particularly valuable when you work with a group of people to validate the product strategy—for example, people from development, marketing, sales, and support. You can improve your Kanban board by adding people's names, deadlines, and maximum effort to the tasks, if necessary; you can also introduce work-in-progress (WIP) limits to optimize the flow of work. Brief daily stand-up meetings—where the people carrying out the validation work come together, stand in front of the Kanban board, and review the status of the tasks—can be very helpful to assess progress and coordinate everyone's work.

Regular Review Meetings

While working with a time box and a Kanban board are helpful techniques, they are not enough. You should also track and review the progress on a regular basis. My preference is to hold weekly review meetings that involve the people carrying out the validation work as well as the management sponsor. Use the meetings to reflect on the risks that are being addressed and the ones that still exist in your product strategy. Review how you are collaborating and identify improvement measures, such as involving someone from finance, improving the Kanban board, pivoting, or even stopping the strategy work immediately if it is no longer possible or beneficial to realize the vision. Ask a ScrumMaster or agile coach to facilitate the meeting when more people are involved, so that you can focus on reviewing progress and identifying improvements.

PART 2: PRODUCT ROADMAP

Good fortune is what happens when opportunity meets with planning.
Thomas Edison

The second part of this book explores a specific strategy practice—product roadmapping—together with a popular and powerful tool called the product roadmap. Product roadmaps translate strategic decisions into actionable plans that provide direction for the development team and the other stakeholders. Roadmaps help everyone involved in making the product a success understand how the product is likely to grow and how this will affect their work.

This part consists of four chapters: Roadmap Foundations, Development, Reviews, and Portfolio Roadmaps. The first chapter covers practices that are essential for successfully employing a product roadmap, including selecting the right roadmapping approach and engaging the right people in the roadmapping process. The second chapter, Roadmap Development, provides techniques that help you get your roadmap right, such as determining dates and cost. The third chapter talks about reviewing and updating the product roadmap to ensure it stays actionable and helpful. The final chapter offers an outlook on portfolio roadmaps to help you manage a group of related products.

ROADMAP FOUNDATIONS

The product roadmap can be an incredibly useful tool for implementing the product strategy and aligning the stakeholders. This chapter equips you with the prerequisites for effectively working with product roadmaps, and it lays the foundations for the rest of this part. It discusses what's at the heart of a roadmap, together with the benefits it provides; which roadmapping approach is best suited for your product, how to create strong buy-in from the stakeholders; how the product roadmap and the product backlog differ, and how you can avoid common roadmapping mistakes.

Why You Need a Product Roadmap

Imagine you have decided to drive to your next holiday destination. Having a strategy to get there by car is all well and good, but it leaves you with a number of unanswered questions: Which specific route should you choose to get there? Should you take highways or country roads? Should you stop off along the way? If so, where and when? Without answering these questions, I would find it daring simply to drive off—certainly with three children in the back of the car.

What's true for a road trip also applies to your product. Having a shared vision and a valid strategy is necessary, but it is not enough. You need to detail the journey you want to take your product on, describe how the strategy is to be executed, and come up with an actionable plan that aligns everyone involved in developing and providing the product. In other words, you need a product roadmap.

In its simplest form, a product roadmap communicates how a product is likely to evolve by mapping its major releases onto a timeline, as Figure 35 shows. A major release is a product version that creates value for the customers or users, such as enhancing the user experience or providing new functionality.

FIGURE 35: The Essential Product Roadmap

Forecasting how your product might grow allows you to connect individual releases. This creates a continuity of purpose, helps you make prioritization decisions, and unburdens the product backlog. And as your product matures and the product strategy stabilizes, you may find that the product roadmap becomes your primary tool for expressing strategic decisions.

While you may also employ a product backlog to describe your product, it is usually too detailed to offer a clear, longer-term outlook. Solely relying on your backlog is like blindly trusting the instructions of your satellite navigation system and not looking at the overall route—something I have learned to avoid after a number of prolonged and unpleasant journeys. (I'll talk more about the relationship between the product roadmap and the backlog in the section "Get the Relationship between the Roadmap and the Product Backlog Right.")

If your development team releases software continuously, you might be wondering if you need a product roadmap at all. While continuous deployments are very useful for smaller fixes and incremental enhancements, a product roadmap reduces the risk of getting lost in a myriad of small changes and no longer seeing the overall direction in which you are heading. When applied correctly, the two techniques can complement each other nicely.

Be Clear on the Different Types and Formats of Product Roadmaps

Product roadmaps come in different shapes and sizes. I find it helpful to distinguish two basic types: *feature-based* roadmaps and *goal-oriented* roadmaps. Feature-based roadmaps are built on product features, such as registration, search, or reporting, which are then mapped onto a timeline to indicate when each feature will be released; a cost-benefit analysis is often used to determine if and when a feature should be implemented. Goal-oriented roadmaps take a different approach. As their name suggests, these roadmaps focus on goals or objectives. Sample goals might include acquiring customers, increasing engagement, and removing technical debt. Features still exist, but they are viewed as second-class citizens; they are derived from the goals and used sparingly, as Figure 36 illustrates.[41]

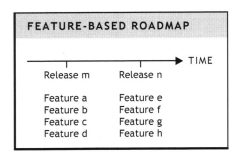 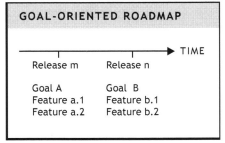

FIGURE 36: Feature-Based vs. Goal-Oriented Roadmap

Product roadmaps also vary depending on their audience. An internal roadmap is visible only within the company that is creating and providing the product. Its main purpose is threefold: to align the stakeholders, to ensure that everybody has the same understanding of how the product is likely to grow, and to help the stakeholders carry out

---

41 As mentioned in Part 1, I view a feature as a product capability. In an agile context, a feature is broken down into epics, which are further divided into user stories.

their work, such as creating the necessary marketing collateral or preparing the sales channels. External roadmaps, in contrast, are visible to the customers and users. Some companies use these roadmaps as a marketing and sales tool, and to demonstrate the company's commitment to the product. You can, of course, work with separate internal and external roadmaps. Just make sure the two are in sync and that the external roadmap doesn't make any promises you might not be able to deliver, for instance, by not showing any dates on your external roadmap.

Product roadmaps commonly use a table that shows the relevant information, including the release dates or time frames, the goals, and the features. (See the section below called "Capture Your Roadmap with the GO Template" for a sample roadmap template.) But there is no reason why you cannot employ a more visual style. You could, for instance, express your roadmap as a storyboard—a sequence of illustrations or images like a brief comic strip. When I worked at Siemens, for instance, the visionary roadmaps were literally pictures that crisply showed the likely trends for a certain industry, such as energy or telecommunications.

When it comes to choosing a roadmapping tool, I prefer to work with a paper-based product roadmap whenever possible. Such a roadmap facilitates collaboration and visualization; it makes it easy for others to contribute to the plan; and putting it up on the wall makes it visible and accessible. But if you decide to work with an electronic product roadmap, start with a simple spreadsheet so that you can easily experiment with different roadmap formats before you decide which (if any) of the commercial tools is right for you. The biggest mistake you can make is to select a tool and hope that it will fix your roadmapping challenges. While this may sound farfetched, I have witnessed product management groups do this—sadly, with poor results.

Choose the Right Roadmapping Approach

While every roadmap should communicate the likely growth of your product, the best roadmapping approach for your product depends on the amount of uncertainty and change present. This is similar to planning a car journey: the better you know the route, the more you can plan ahead in detail and correctly anticipate what's ahead. But if you are traveling on a new route, you are likely to lack detailed knowledge and stick to a few key milestones, such as where to exit a highway or where to stop overnight.

In order to select the right roadmapping approach, consider the maturity of your product and the stability of its market. The younger your product is, the more uncertainty and change are likely to be present. Young products benefit from a high-level roadmap that focuses on product goals or benefits, such as increasing engagement or retaining customers, that does not look too far ahead, and that is frequently reviewed and updated. But older, more mature products lend themselves to more detailed roadmaps that cover longer time frames and require fewer reviews. The reason for this is simple: as your product reaches maturity, it will experience fewer changes, and you will be in a better position to correctly anticipate its growth.

In addition to your product's age, look at the stability of the target market. If your product is mature but its market or market segment is volatile—for example, if competitors keep adding new features or if the technologies are in flux—you will have to update your product to keep it attractive and defend its market share. As a consequence, uncertainty and change will creep back into your roadmap. This makes it difficult to plan ahead in detail and correctly forecast when each detailed feature will be released. Instead, you are probably better off creating a higher-level roadmap that focuses on product goals. Taking into account product maturity and market stability results in the roadmap selection matrix shown in Figure 37.

FIGURE 37: Roadmap Selection Matrix

Figure 37 captures the maturity of your product on the vertical axis and the stability of its market on the horizontal axis. By distinguishing young and mature products and dynamic and stable markets, four quadrants emerge that help you choose the appropriate format, planning horizon, and review frequency for your roadmap. As Figure 37 shows, I recommend using a goal-oriented product roadmap when your product and/or your market are likely to change. If your product is young and your market is dynamic, then you should keep your roadmap coarse-grained, limit the planning horizon to about six months, and stay away from detailed features. Instead, focus on the benefits your product should deliver—for instance, acquiring new customers or reducing cost—and review your roadmap every four weeks. If your product is mature but the market is volatile, or if your product is young but the market is stable, then I also recommend working with a goal-oriented roadmap, but you can add more features, extend the planning horizon, and decrease the review frequency to once per quarter. If your product has reached maturity and the market is stable or has started to decline, then a feature-based roadmap that is more detailed and looks ahead further is likely to work well. Reviewing the roadmap every three to six months should be sufficient.

As your product and your market change, so should your roadmap; the more uncertainty and change are present, the more frequently you should review and update your roadmap. More extensive changes to your product may cause you to change the roadmapping approach. For example, rejuvenating a mature product may cause you to switch from a feature-based roadmap to a goal-oriented one.[42] But if your roadmap changes too frequently—say, on a weekly basis— then it will become unusable, and the stakeholders are likely to lose trust in it. It is therefore important that you plan ahead only as far as you can realistically see, and capture only what you can confidently anticipate.

Understand Who Benefits from Your Roadmap

As mentioned in Part 1, achieving product success requires more than building a great product. In order to create truly successful products, people from different business groups have to work together. Your product roadmap should facilitate this collaboration. It should create a *shared* understanding of how your product is likely to grow so that the stakeholders can plan their work accordingly and contribute to the product's success. This may involve selecting the right marketing mix, creating the sales collateral, and preparing the target environment. This is similar to planning a family road trip: I've learned that understanding everyone's needs and interests is a good idea. Unhappy

---

42　For more information on the product life cycle stages, please refer to Part 1.

family members make the car journey rather unpleasant. Think of the stakeholders as the roadmap users. Figure 38 shows a set of sample stakeholders.

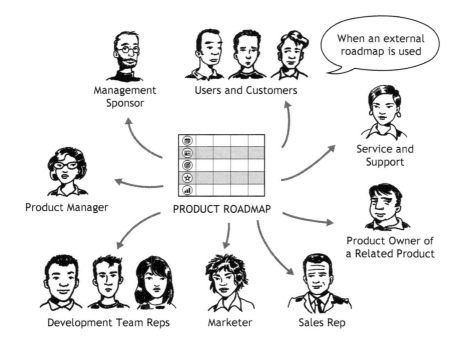

FIGURE 38: The Product Roadmap and the Stakeholders

Depending on the type of your product, the stakeholders will vary more or less from the ones shown in Figure 38. For an in-house product, such as a data warehouse application, you will probably have the operations group as roadmap stakeholders instead of marketing, sales, and customer support.[43] Table 7 takes a closer look at the different stakeholders and their expectations.

---

43 See the section "Engage the Stakeholders" in Part 1 for more information on stakeholder identification and analysis.

TABLE 7: The Stakeholders and Their Expectations
of the Product Roadmap

Stakeholder	Expectations
Product manager	• Communicate how the product strategy is implemented and how the product is likely to grow. • Provide direction and guidance to the stakeholders; get the stakeholders to agree on the plan and to contribute to the individual releases. • Obtain management approval and acquire a budget; set and manage management expectations. • Track the success of the individual releases to proactively manage the product.
Management sponsor	• Ensure that the product implements the right strategic goals and that the product roadmap and the company strategy are aligned. • Measure and track the product performance to understand if the product delivers, i.e., if the money spent on it is a worthwhile investment. • Agree on an appropriate budget.
Development team	• Understand what's ahead; influence the roadmap to take into account, for instance, technology changes, user experience concerns, and technical debt. • Make sure the roadmap is feasible and that the team can design and build the product; allocate the right people.
Marketing and sales	• Anticipate the necessary work to market and sell the product; create the right marketing campaign, train the sales staff, and develop the necessary marketing and sales collateral. • Ensure that the work can be done and allocate the right people. • Influence the roadmap so that marketing and sales concerns are taken into account.
Product and portfolio management	• Anticipate and manage dependencies. • Coordinate releases across different products.
Customers and users	• Influence the product—for instance, change goals and add features. • Prepare for new releases and make sure that the organization is ready to take advantage of them.

As Table 7 shows, your product roadmap should guide the work of the various stakeholders. It should be a feasible plan that aligns everyone involved in making the product a success. A good way to achieve this is to create, review, and update the roadmap collaboratively, as I discuss in more detail in the next section.

Involve the Stakeholders

No matter how well thought-out your product roadmap is, it is worthless if the key stakeholders or players don't support it. A great way to achieve organizational alignment and strong buy-in from these stakeholders is to involve them in a collaborative workshop. This leverages their ideas and knowledge; it ensures that the roadmap is feasible and that people agree with it; and it lets the stakeholders hear one another's ideas and requests, which saves you from having to act as a go-between, trying to broker compromises between the individuals.[44] If the stakeholders are in different locations, I recommend inviting them to an on-site workshop, as the most effective method of conveying information in product development is still face-to-face conversation. Ask your ScrumMaster or coach to help you with booking and setting up an appropriate room, setting the ground rules, and facilitating the workshop so that you can focus on shaping the roadmap.

Start the workshop by briefly reviewing the product strategy. Ideally, the workshop participants will have been involved in creating and testing the strategy and will already be familiar with it. Two to four hours should be enough to create a roadmap with measurable goals, dates, key features, and metrics. If you need significantly more time, then chances are there is something wrong with your strategy, or not all attendees are willing to buy into it or collaborate. The outcome of the workshop should be a product roadmap that is shared and actionable—agreed by everyone and ready to be put into practice.

While a collaborative roadmapping approach can be very helpful, you should make sure that you lead the roadmapping work and influence the creation of the product roadmap. Roadmapping means making product decisions, which can be tough calls. Your roadmap should not be the smallest common denominator, but should translate the product strategy into a meaningful and actionable plan, and it should

---

44 While the capabilities and the capacity of the development group often affect if creating a new product or feature is possible, I have seen organizations where marketing, legal, or another business group was the bottleneck, and hence determined the roadmap's feasibility.

tell a cohesive story about the likely growth of your product. While it is normal that this will involve some negotiation and compromise, not everyone will necessarily be happy with every detail in the roadmap. That's fine, as long as people agree with the overall plan. Similarly, don't allow powerful stakeholders to dominate and take control of the roadmap. Don't say yes to every idea or request, as this will turn your roadmap into a feature soup: a random collection of features. Use the product strategy to make the right decisions. Be strong and have the courage to say no if necessary. Ask the ScrumMaster to establish the ground rules and facilitate the workshop so that you can concentrate on creating the roadmap.

Once the product roadmap is available, you should continue to involve the stakeholders on a regular basis and invite them to review and update the roadmap, as I describe in more detail later in this part. It is best if the same individuals should continue to be involved in the road-mapping activities, as this creates continuity, avoids handoffs and loss of knowledge, and facilitates effective collaboration.

Get the Relationship between the Roadmap and the Product Backlog Right

As mentioned earlier, the product roadmap and the product backlog are two important product management tools. Each tool has its own strengths and weaknesses. While the product roadmap is a strategic high-level plan that describes how your product is likely to develop across several product releases, the product backlog is a tactical tool that contains the items necessary to create one or more releases. These items include epics, user stories, nonfunctional requirements, design sketches, and other artifacts that describe what the product should do and look like. Both tools nicely complement each other when applied properly, as Figure 39 shows.[45]

---

45   For more information on the product backlog, see Pichler (2010).

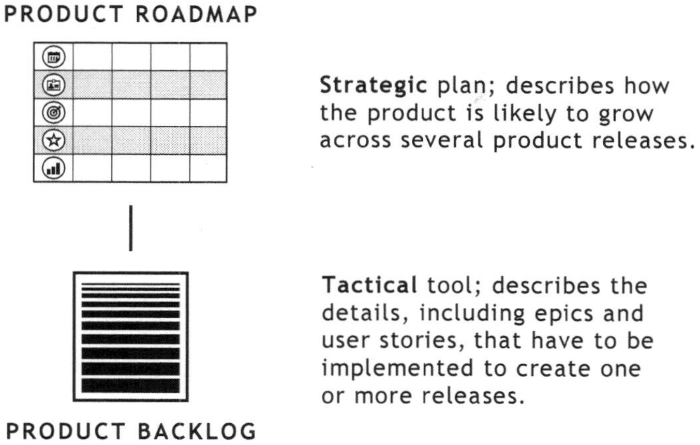

PRODUCT ROADMAP

Strategic plan; describes how
the product is likely to grow
across several product releases.

Tactical tool; describes the
details, including epics and
user stories, that have to be
implemented to create one
or more releases.

PRODUCT BACKLOG

FIGURE 39: Product Roadmap and Product Backlog

Unfortunately, I find that product roadmaps sometimes contain too
many details, including epics and user stories, and that some product
backlogs look too far into the future. This blurs the line between the
two artifacts; it results in a product roadmap that is difficult to understand, prone to change, and overly long and hard to manage. You should
thus keep the two tools separate and leverage their respective strengths.
Employ the roadmap to describe your product's overall journey and the
backlog to capture the details. Adopting this approach helped one of
my clients, a major games studio, reduce its product backlog from over
a thousand items to less than one hundred.

I also recommend that you derive the product backlog from your
roadmap, particularly when your product is still young or the market
is dynamic. You can take this approach further and focus your product
backlog on the next product release. This creates a concise backlog that
is easier to update and change by using the feedback and data generated
as you expose product increments to the customers and users.[46] What's
more, every sprint should take you a step closer to the next release.

46 A *product increment* is usually defined as working software that can be shipped
to the customers and users. But as it is a step toward the final product, a prod-

Be aware, though, that the product backlog also influences the product roadmap: the feedback you receive from exposing product increments to customers and users may lead to roadmap adjustments, for instance. Similarly, if the work in the sprints does not progress as anticipated, you may have to update the roadmap and modify, for example, the goal or the date. It is therefore important that you keep the product roadmap and the product backlog in sync.

Avoid These Common Roadmapping Mistakes

While the product roadmap is a helpful tool, I find that it is not always used effectively. Watch out for the three common roadmapping mistakes discussed below.

No Guarantee

A product roadmap is not a guarantee; it is a high-level plan that describes the likely growth of your product based on what you currently know. It's good to have confidence in your roadmap, and it is great to be committed to your product. But your product roadmap is not fixed; it will change. Review and update the roadmap regularly, and involve the key stakeholders in the roadmapping activities to ensure that they understand and support the product roadmap. Choose the right roadmap format and the right level of detail to avoid making more roadmapping changes than are necessary. As discussed earlier, a goal-oriented roadmap is particularly useful when your product or market is changing.

---

uct increment might also be a throwaway prototype that addresses a product risk—for example, if users are willing to register first before they can use the product (user experience risk), or if the design of the data access layer is efficient enough (technical risk). The product increment in the former case might be a paper prototype; the increment in the latter example is likely to be a spike, or technical prototype. Product increments therefore help to validate the product and incrementally enhance it by adding new functionality and improving existing features.

No Speculation

Don't create a roadmap if you don't have a valid product strategy available or if you cannot look beyond the first public release. You should not attempt to create a roadmap if you cannot confidently answer who the product is for, why people would want to buy and use it, why they would choose it over a competing offer, if it is feasible to build the product, why it is worthwhile for your business to invest in it, and if it is economically viable to develop and provide the product. Instead of rushing to build a roadmap, recognize that you have to first work on the product strategy, as I explained in Part 1.

Being able to look beyond the next release means that you can realistically anticipate the longer-term growth of your product. If you are working on a brand-new product, for instance, and are about to launch your first minimum viable product (MVP), you may not be in a position to create a realistic product roadmap for the next twelve months. Delay the creation of the roadmap until you have a valid product strategy in place. Otherwise, you are likely to end up with a speculative, unreliable, and useless roadmap that provides little value to the people involved in achieving product success. In the worst case, people will lose trust in the product roadmap as a planning tool and will doubt your ability to plan ahead.

No Epics and User Stories

A user story is a brief narrative that describes product functionality from the perspective of the users; it is usually small enough to be implemented within a few days or weeks. An epic is much bigger and describes a larger piece of functionality; you can think of it as a placeholder for several user stories. Over time an epic is broken down into a number of smaller stories using the data obtained from exposing product increments to customers and users.

While a product roadmap should communicate how a product is likely to evolve, you refrain from including epics and user stories in the plan, as this has several drawbacks: It clutters your roadmap and makes it hard to see how you want your product to progress; it makes it more difficult to achieve agreement with the stakeholders; it is more prone to change; it carries the risk of turning the roadmap into a tactical tool that competes with the product backlog; and it restricts the freedom of the development team to make a commitment and pull the right amount of work into the sprint (assuming that Scrum is used to develop the product). Capture the epics and the user stories in the product backlog, not in the product roadmap. Use the roadmap to describe the big picture and the backlog to describe the details, as I discussed in the section "Get the Relationship between the Roadmap and the Product Backlog Right."

ROADMAP DEVELOPMENT

Creating a realistic product roadmap that is an actionable plan can be challenging. The practices described in this chapter help you address this challenge. They provide guidance on working with release goals, identifying the right release contents, estimating cost, determining release dates, managing dependencies, and determining the success of the releases.

Make Your Product Roadmap SMART

Regardless of the roadmapping approach you choose, you will benefit from a SMART product roadmap: a roadmap whose releases are specific, measurable, agreed, realistic, and time-bound.[47] This will ensure that the roadmap is an actionable plan that guides the work of the development team and the other stakeholders.

Specific
Your product roadmap is *specific* if everyone involved in making the product a success understands what the releases are about and why it is worthwhile to develop them. Bear in mind that your ability to correctly forecast how your product will develop decreases the further you plan ahead. Only add as much detail as you can realistically anticipate while still ensuring that the roadmap contents are clear. Working with goals addresses this challenge, as I explain in more detail in the next section.

---

47   Note that I have replaced the common SMART criterion *achievable* with *agreed*.

Measurable
The roadmap is *measurable* if you can determine if the release has reached its goal and delivered the desired benefits. Including metrics in your product roadmap helps you make the releases measurable.

Agreed
The product roadmap is *agreed* if the stakeholders, including the development team, buy into it. As mentioned earlier, involving the stakeholders in creating, reviewing, and updating the product roadmap generates strong support and ensures that the roadmap is agreed.

Realistic
The roadmap is *realistic* if it is a feasible plan that guides the work of the development team and the other stakeholders. Involving the stakeholders in the roadmapping work will help you recognize if, for example, the development team lacks the necessary skills, or if the marketing group is too stretched to support a release.

Time-Bound
The product roadmap uses dates or time frames to show when each release will be available. The more uncertainty and change are present, and the further you look into the future, the more advisable it is to use time frames rather than specific dates. But this criterion might *not* be helpful for an external roadmap, where stating dates might create unrealistic expectations and put you under pressure to deliver a specific benefit or set of features at a certain point in time. As mentioned before, you may therefore choose to show the order of the major releases on an external roadmap but not specific dates or time frames.

Take Advantage of Release Goals

One of the challenges in creating a realistic roadmap is the change and uncertainty present in digital products. It seems that most of the time, the user experience design, the features, the technologies, and/or the market are changing; all four are sometimes in flux. Faced with this dilemma, you have three choices: First, you can do without a roadmap. Second, you can use a feature-based roadmap with a "likely to change" bumper sticker on it. Third, you can choose a goal-oriented roadmap that focuses on the desired benefits of future releases. Not employing a roadmap is usually not an option for larger companies—unless you cannot see beyond the very next release. Without at least a rough understanding of how the product is likely to grow, the stakeholders can't anticipate and coordinate their work effectively. Similarly, creating an unreliable, feature-based roadmap defeats the purpose: it doesn't allow the stakeholders to plan or carry out their work. Repeatedly making significant changes to a roadmap can also cause the stakeholders to lose trust and to deprioritize your product. Luckily, goal-oriented roadmaps are a helpful alternative.

As mentioned earlier, a goal-oriented roadmap is built on goals like acquiring customers, retaining them, increasing engagement, activating users, generating revenue, future-proofing the product by removing technical debt, or reducing cost. Such a roadmap shows when each goal will be met. Building on the healthy-eating example from Part 1, I could decide, for example, that the app's first release should focus on acquiring and activating users. This would allow me to gather data and learn more about when and how people use the product, in addition to putting the prerequisites in place for generating revenue through in-app purchases (assuming that freemium is used as the business model). You can think of the goals as the justification for creating new product releases. Once you have identified one or more goals, check that each goal does state the reason for creating the release. Don't fall into the trap of stating *features* instead of *goals*: for instance, performance enhancements and bug fixes are not goals, but features. To avoid this mistake, ask *why* it is worthwhile to create the release—for example, to improve the user experience and increase engagement.

Applied properly, a goal-oriented roadmap provides a number of benefits: It helps shift the conversation from debating individual features to establishing shared product goals, and it is less prone to change and more reliable than a feature-based one. Shared goals also facilitate collaboration: they focus everyone on the desired benefits, rather than being fixated on single features. Finally, goals can make it easier to market and sell your product, as they describe the benefits the product creates.

Capture Your Roadmap with the GO Template

Getting the roadmap format right and expressing goals and benefits effectively can be tricky. To help you develop your product roadmap, I have created a goal-oriented roadmap template called the GO Product Roadmap. It is built on the idea that goals are more important than features, and it consists of five elements: date, name, goal, features, and metrics, as Figure 40 shows.

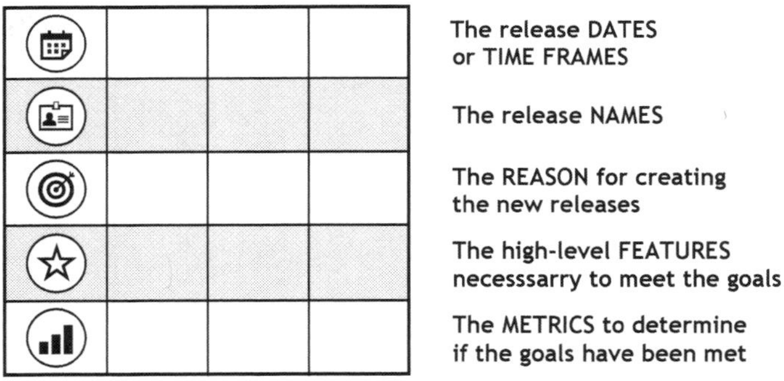

FIGURE 40: The GO Product Roadmap Template

Let's take a look at the rows of the GO roadmap in Figure 40 from top to bottom. The first row captures the *date* or the *time frame* when a new product release should be available—for example, 1 March 2015, or first quarter 2015. The second row states the *name* of the release. Think of release names such as iOS9 or Windows 10, for instance. The third row is the most important part of the GO roadmap. As its name suggests, it states the *goal* of a release, the benefit it should provide, and the reason for creating it. Sample goals include acquiring users, improving the user experience, and removing technical debt. The fourth row lists the product's *features* that are necessary to meet the goal. Derive the features from the goals and ensure that they help create the desired benefits. Focus on what really counts; limit yourself to five features per release, and keep the features coarse-grained. More details, including epics and user stories, are provided in your product backlog. Remember, the purpose of a release is to meet the goal and create the desired benefit, not to deliver features. The fifth and final row captures the *metrics* to determine if a release goal has been met—for example, x amount of users employ the product for at least thirty minutes per day within two weeks after the release becomes available. Stating the metrics ensures that the goals on your roadmap are specific and measurable.

In order to apply the GO roadmap, list the future releases with their dates, names, goals, features, and metrics in the second, third, and fourth columns in Figure 40. You may remove and add columns depending on how many product releases you want to cover. If the GO roadmap format resonates with you, then download it from my website, where you can find more information about it. You can, of course, re-create it using your favorite roadmapping tool, such as an electronic spreadsheet or a flip chart. Feel free to tailor it to your specific needs. You might add the marketing and sales channels for specific releases to your product roadmap, for example, or you could include cost targets if the individual releases must adhere to a specific budget. But make sure that the resulting roadmap is still based on the goals your product should meet.

Determine the Right Release Contents

When you define the releases on your product roadmap, strive for a plan that tells a realistic and coherent story about the likely growth of your product. Your roadmap should not contain a random sequence of releases or a loose collection of features. Instead, it should be an actionable plan that implements the product strategy in such a way that each release builds on the previous one and moves your product closer to the vision. To put it differently, the releases on the roadmap should be stepping-stones toward your vision; they should help you execute the product strategy and move the product forward.

For new products or bigger product updates, such as unbundling a feature or taking a product to a new market, ask yourself what it would take to implement the product strategy. Leverage the insights gained from validating the strategy to decide how you can best translate the strategy into a series of releases that will create value for the customers and users or for your business. In the case of my new healthy-eating app, the first releases could focus on user acquisition and activation, retention, and revenue generation (again, assuming that freemium is the business model I use). As this example shows, the business model can be helpful for determining the releases for a new product.

For existing products, use the key performance indicators (KPIs) to shape the product roadmap. Look for areas where your product does not perform well, and address them in your plan. If engagement is declining, for instance, then you may want to focus one or more releases on improving this indicator by adding a new feature, enhancing an existing one, or providing performance and stability improvements. If the product health is degrading and the software is becoming more difficult to extend and maintain, you should consider an architecture refactoring release. Make sure that you have the right KPIs in place and collect the right data, as discussed in Part 1. If you don't know how the product is performing or if the strategy is working, then it will be difficult to get the roadmap right.

Prelaunch Releases
Showing prelaunch releases can be helpful if you require more than six months to ship a first minimal product. A good practice is to structure longer development efforts in quarters and have quarterly goals on your roadmap. This does not mean, of course, that you have to wait until the end of a quarter to release software. Instead, it suggests that you should release software at least every quarter.

Get the Features on Your Roadmap Right

Most product roadmaps come with features—with good reason: goals alone are usually not enough to understand what needs to be done to successfully deliver a release. To get the features on your roadmap right, start by making them high level. Ensure that they are product capabilities or deliverables; examples include "track what I eat" or "evaluate the food consumed" for my healthy-eating app. Don't make the features on your product roadmap too detailed. Otherwise it will become difficult to see how your product should evolve, and your roadmap will overlap too much with the product backlog. Don't mistake epics or user stories for "features." A feature is a product capability. You can think of it as a group of epics.

Goal-Oriented vs. Feature-Based Roadmaps

On a goal-oriented roadmap, features exist to meet a goal and generate a benefit. You should therefore state the goals first and then derive the features from the goals. To put it differently, goals come first, features second. As mentioned before, I recommend that you don't use more than five features per goal, and avoid adding features altogether when your planning accuracy is low. When you work with a feature-based roadmap, however, features are first-class citizens that you directly add to the appropriate releases. They may originate from customer requests, user forum messages, or solution interviews, for example.

Cost-Benefit Analysis

No matter which roadmap type you are using, perform a cost-benefit analysis if you are unsure whether you should add a feature to the product roadmap. Ask the development team to estimate the rough effort required to provide the feature. High-level relative estimates, such as story points, are often sufficient to get an indication of the cost. Then determine the likely impact. What benefit is the feature likely to provide? What is the risk that you take if you *don't* implement the feature? If you are using a goal-oriented roadmap, find the release goal the feature supports, and determine the feature's impact on achieving the goal. If no corresponding goal exists, explore if it is worthwhile to change your roadmap and adjust an existing goal, or if you should introduce a new goal so that the feature can be added to the roadmap.

For a feature-based product roadmap, consider how the feature affects the product performance. Let's look at an example. Say my healthy-eating app has become a mature product, and I now need to decide between two features: enhance the responsiveness of the product, or increase its stability. In order to make the right decision, I would consider which feature is likely to have a bigger impact on the product success, including retaining customers and defending market share. If you have to choose between several features, select the one that gives you the biggest bang for your buck, as they say.

Adding New Features

While it's great to come up with new ideas and features, don't blindly add them to your roadmap. This not only clutters your plan, but turns your product into a feature soup, which, as noted earlier, is a loose collection of largely unrelated features. Instead, ensure that every feature helps you move the product in the right direction. Combine features into coherent, well-rounded releases, even for feature-based roadmaps. This makes it easier to communicate how the product is likely to develop and to understand if the release is successful.

If a stakeholder requests a feature, then ask why the feature is important and how it helps the product create value. If you get a lot of pressure from stakeholders to implement specific features, this can be an indication that they don't understand or support the product roadmap. If that's the case, reflect on how you engage the stakeholders and explore how you can improve those relationships.

Identify the Success Factors

In an ideal world, the product roadmap allows the development team to deliver all the releases on time, meet all the goals, provide all the features, and adhere to the agreed budget. But in reality, product-development efforts don't always go smoothly, and unforeseen things do happen. As Murphy's Law states: "Anything that can go wrong, will go wrong."[48] The development progress may not be as fast as anticipated, for instance, or one of the technologies may not be usable. It is therefore important that you understand which aspect has the biggest impact on the success of your product so that you can protect it. Is it delivering the release contents, releasing on time, or adhering to the budget? This factor is also called the *primary success factor* (Kerzner 2013).

Identifying the Primary Success Factor

Sometimes the primary success factor is obvious. If you know, for example, that your product must be ready for Christmas or a major tradeshow, then on-time delivery is a must and hence your primary success factor. Similarly, if you have a fixed budget, then cost is your primary success factor. If you are unsure, then carry out an impact analysis. Ask yourself if releasing late—partially meeting the release goal, or not delivering all features—or overrunning the budget would have the worst impact on the product performance. Say that I am going on a road trip with my family and we have prebooked a hotel to stay in overnight. Getting to the hotel would then be my primary success factor. Not making it to the hotel and having to spend the night in the car would be worse than arriving late (assuming our rooms are secured), spending more money on gasoline and toll roads, or risking a speeding fine.

Protecting the Primacy Success Factor

Once you have found the primary success factor, you must protect it. If it's on-time delivery, for example, then do everything in your power to ensure that your product is shipped on schedule. Consider the first iPhone. In order to ensure that the product would be released on time, Apple was prepared to partially implement some features and to increase cost by adding more people to the development effort. The very first release shipped without the ability to send text messages to multi-

---

48   See http://en.wikipedia.org/wiki/Murphy's_law.

ple recipients, for instance, which is something every ordinary mobile phone at the time could do. As this example shows, protecting the primary success factor requires you to relax at least one other factor.

The Iron Triangle and the Secondary Success Factor

A handy tool for illustrating that release contents, date, and budget cannot be fixed simultaneously is the Iron Triangle. Traditionally, the triangle looks at scope, time, and budget. To optimize it for developing a roadmap, I have replaced *scope* with *goal or features* in Figure 41.

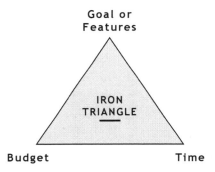

FIGURE 41: The Revised Iron Triangle

The Iron Triangle states that one of its vertices must stay flexible and act as a release valve to account for unforeseen events. You cannot lock down all three factors—unless you compromise quality, which is not advisable. Compromising quality may give you some short-term benefits, like an increased development velocity, but it will hurt you in the long run. If your product suffers from poor quality, users may get frustrated and stop using it. In addition, responding to changes and adapting the product will take longer and be more expensive. Therefore, don't flex quality, but keep it fixed.[49]

---

49   As I discussed in Part 1, you should consider making software quality one of your KPIs. This will ensure that you don't overlook the architecture refactoring work necessary to keep your product healthy and be able to change the software quickly.

The primary success factor not only helps you focus on what matters most, it also helps you determine the other two factors:

- If the date is fixed, find out to what extent you can achieve the goal, and how many people with which skills are required to come up with a rough budget.
- If the goal is fixed, determine how long it is likely to take to achieve the goal, or how long you can wait to launch the product (the window of opportunity, discussed in the next section); identify how many people you need with which skills.
- If the budget is fixed, determine to what extent you can meet the goal and how much time this is likely to take you, or how long you can wait to have the release available.

To help you make the right trade-off decisions between the two non-primary factors, determine the *secondary success factor*, which is the one with the second biggest impact on the product success. Take the road-trip example from above. Getting to the hotel before dinner would be my secondary success factor. While going to bed hungry is not quite as bad as having to spend the night in the car, I would rather increase cost and speed up the journey than sleep with a rumbling tummy.

Multiple Releases

When you create your product roadmap, determine if all releases share the same primary and secondary success factors, or if they differ. For a new product development effort, for example, you may have to create an initial minimal product (i.e., the primary factor) to be able to launch and do your best to release the product by a certain date or within a certain time frame (the secondary factor). For the next few releases, however, you may want to swap the factors. Delivering on time might become the primary success factor, and fully reaching the release goals the secondary one (assuming that you can flex the budget).

Brooks' Law

Be aware that increasing the budget to add more people to the development effort should be planned carefully. It should not be a fire-fighting measure. As Brooks' law states, "Adding manpower to a late software project makes it later."[50] It may take time to recruit the right people, and then they will need to get up to speed before they can be productive. It also takes some time for a group of individuals to become a true team: a tightly knit unit with members who trust and support one another and work together effectively.[51] As a consequence, when you add people to the development team, productivity usually drops before it increases. In reality, you are often faced with trading off date and goal/features, and you will then have to decide if you should adhere to the date but flex the scope, or if you should fully meet the goal and deliver all features but postpone the release date.

Balance or Pivot?

Balancing the contents, the dates, and the budget for all the releases may require you to iterate your product roadmap, particularly when you are making bigger changes to your product. But if you cannot achieve an acceptable trade-off, then your product strategy may not be executable; you may have to pivot. To build on the road-trip example, if you cannot get to the destination at an acceptable time and on a realistic budget, then you will have to consider an alternative, such as traveling by plane or train. If that's the case for your product, then you should stop the product roadmap work and go back to the drawing board. Look for a new product strategy and carry out the necessary validation before you create a new roadmap.

---

50   See https://en.wikipedia.org/wiki/Brooks'_law.
51   See, for example, Tuckman (1965). While more recent models offer more stages than Tuckman's, the basic insight remains the same: a group of people has to go through a team-building process before the individuals will be able to work together effectively.

Determine the Window of Opportunity

In order to figure out when a product can be released, people traditionally investigate how long it will take to get the work done. Requirements are compiled; work packages, tasks, and dependencies are identified; and estimates are made based on how long each task might take. The tasks are added up and a delivery date appears. But I find that *how long* is often the wrong question to ask.

A better and much faster way to identify the dates on your roadmap is to investigate the date at which the releases must be available in order to achieve the desired benefits. This time frame is called the *window of opportunity* (Wysocki 2013). Say I want to determine the release dates for my healthy-eating app. Since the market for mobile health apps is rapidly evolving at the time of writing, I should aim to launch sooner rather than later and have the first version available in three to six months. Even if the product is just good enough and rather minimal, releasing something soon will allow me to get a foot in the door, acquire users, and then learn how they use the product so that I can adapt it accordingly.

As this example shows, the window of opportunity is particularly helpful when you develop a new product or when you make a bigger change to an existing one, such as taking it to a new market or rejuvenating it. The amount of uncertainty present in both cases makes it very difficult, if not impossible, to employ a traditional approach by breaking features into epics and user stories that will be detailed enough to estimate them correctly.

To get the window of opportunity right, you have to know how dynamic and fast-paced your market is. Is it changing quickly, or is it fairly stable? If you have done some initial validation work and carried out some competitor research, for instance, you should be able to answer this question and choose the right time frame. Once you have started building the product, track the actual progress in order to understand if the time window is realistic or not, as I describe later in more detail in the section "Track the Progress."

Use a Steady Release Cadence,
but Break It When Necessary

A *steady release cadence* means releasing software at a set rhythm—for example, every two weeks in the case of the Facebook mobile app, or every six weeks in the case of the Google Chrome browser.[52] You essentially timebox your releases and choose the same length for all of them. As mentioned before, however, you can and should deliver small improvements and bug fixes continuously.

Employing a steady release cadence provides you with three benefits: First, it simplifies and improves the planning process. As the date is fixed, you can focus on setting the right goals and sizing them so they fit into the time boxes. If the cadence is high and you ship new releases frequently, you will learn how much you can actually achieve within a time box and you will get better at setting realistic goals. Second, your customers will see that the product is regularly enhanced and that more value is being provided to them. They will also know when a new version is being released, and that it will be available on time; if you have customers who want a feature that did *not* make it into the latest releases, waiting for the next release will usually be acceptable to them as long as you provide new releases frequently. Third, a high release cadence can give you a competitive advantage. New competitors (so-called *insurgents*) will have to match your pace.

A steady release cadence can be particularly helpful once your product has stabilized and you begin to focus on incremental improvements to penetrate the market or defend market share. Take, for instance, the Google Chrome browser. It took Google about two years to develop version 1.0, which the company released in December 2008. For the next two years, the Chrome team released a new version about every four to six months. Since then, a new version has been released every six weeks.[53] By the time Google reached its six-week cadence, the product

---

52   A steady release cadence is sometimes also referred to as a "release train."
53   See http://en.wikipedia.org/wiki/Timeline_of_web_browsers.

was well into the growth stage and had become the third biggest browser in terms of usage share.[54]

But a steady release cadence is not always beneficial. For example, if you are planning to make a bigger change to your product in order to get it ready for the growth stage, take it to a new market, or alter some of the underlying technologies, then you should plan for the necessary validation work. You may have to observe and interview people, carry out some competitor analysis, or build MVPs and spikes (as described in Part 1) before you can start developing the new version. Your product roadmap may therefore look similar to the one shown in Figure 42.

FIGURE 42: Roadmap with Validation and Development Work

As the sample roadmap in Figure 42 shows, the time required to ship *Release o* is considerably longer compared to the other releases. This is due to the validation work required. Once *Release o* becomes available, a shorter and steady release cadence is resumed. If you want to be able to anticipate the right validation effort, you should take into account the risks and unknowns that are present and consider timeboxing the validation work, as I discussed in more detail in Part 1.

While you are working on *Release o*, you should still aim to release software early and frequently—but only to an appropriate test group. In the case of the Google Chrome browser, other Google employees received a new build every week for test purposes long before the first public release was available. This allowed the Chrome team to collect data and feedback early on, and helped drive the product forward (Fisher 2008).

---

54 See http://en.wikipedia.org/wiki/Usage_share_of_web_browsers.

Determine the Cost

Before you decide to go on a road trip, you probably want to know how much the journey is likely to cost. If money matters, you may also choose the cheapest route, avoiding toll roads along the way, for example. If you know the vehicle you'll be driving and you have tools like Google Maps available, you can easily determine the distance, road fees, gas consumption, and any other cost factors so that you can calculate a reliable cost estimate. But imagine traveling through uncharted territory or through regions where no detailed maps are available. In that case, the same approach would not work well, as you'd lack the necessary data to determine the cost. Instead, you could choose a different approach and compare the journey to other trips you have taken to derive a rough cost estimate by analogy. While this initial estimate is likely to be a ballpark figure, it should be good enough to make the right decision: Should you use the route, adjust it, or opt for another one? Or should you even change your strategy and reconsider other options, such as traveling by plane or by train? Once you are on your way, you could measure the actual gas consumption and the road fees to determine if your initial high-level estimate was roughly right, and take any corrective actions as needed.

Precise and Correct Estimates vs. Rough Approximations

Determining the cost required to implement a product roadmap is similar to planning a road trip. If your product is mature, if you have a detailed and stable product backlog available, if the development team can correctly estimate the backlog items, and if you can accurately anticipate the team's velocity, you will be able to calculate a precise and correct cost estimate up front.[55] But if your product is new, young, or changing, you will be in unfamiliar territory, and employing the same approach will not work well. You may struggle to break the roadmap features into epics and user stories, your team may not be able to esti-

---

55 This assumes that your development team uses common agile estimation techniques such as story points, ideal days, and Planning Poker. For more information, see Cohn (2005).

mate the items correctly, and you won't be able to accurately anticipate the velocity and keep the backlog stable. Even if you manage to make it work, you will end up with an overly long and complex product backlog that is difficult to adjust and maintain. What's more, it can take days—and in some cases weeks—to turn the features into well-defined requirements and to come up with detailed estimates.

But are detailed estimates really required at this stage? Let's look at the two main reasons for determining the cost in the context of the product roadmap. The first one is to ensure that developing the product is economically sensible and the right thing to do. Knowing the amount also helps allocate a realistic budget and manage cash flow. The second reason is to ensure that the roadmap is feasible, and that enough people with the right skills are available to design, implement, and test the product. To meet these two objectives, I generally find it sufficient to determine how many people with which skills are likely to be required to create the desired releases on the roadmap. To apply this approach, draw on your experience of developing similar products or previous versions of the same product; consider whether enough people with the right expertise are available in your company, or if you will have to hire or contract people. This should give you an indication of the likely labor cost required, as Figure 43 shows. Then add the cost for facilities, infrastructure, materials, licenses, and other relevant items. Carry out this exercise together with the development team.

Product Roadmap   How many people with which skills?   Rough Estimate

FIGURE 43: Determining a Rough Initial Cost Estimate

The resulting estimate will be rough, as you cannot anticipate in detail what needs to be done to deliver the individual releases. But that's OK as long as it is *good enough* to make a go/no-go decision. After all, "it is better to be roughly right than to be precisely wrong," as the economist John Maynard Keynes said. Better yet, determining the budget along the lines described is fast: you could even do it in a product roadmapping workshop, as discussed in the section "Involve the Stakeholders." A good way to express the uncertainty inherently attached to your estimate is to use a range: for instance, $50–70K, $150–250K, or $2–3 million. If you have a fixed, predetermined budget, or if you cannot adjust an existing development team, ask the team members if they are confident that they can deliver the releases within the desired time frame.

Taking Action

If the resulting budget is too high, or if the team considers the roadmap to be unrealistic, then you have two options: persevere and adjust your roadmap or pivot and search for a more cost-effective and feasible strategy. Figure 44 summarizes these options.

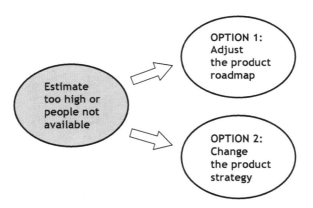

FIGURE 44: Pivot or Persevere?

Once you have started developing the product, you should track the progress and the actual expenditures in order to understand if the initial cost estimate is realistic or not, as I describe later in more detail in the section "Track the Progress."

Take Dependencies into Account

Creating an actionable product roadmap requires you to take dependencies into account. These come in three flavors: dependencies between individual releases of your product, dependencies on people, and dependencies on other products. Let's look at these three types of dependencies in turn and discuss how you can deal with them.

Between Releases

I find it common that architecture refactorings must be implemented before new features can be added. An interesting example is Apple's Mac OS X Snow Leopard, which was released in 2009, after nearly two years of work. While Snow Leopard didn't provide new functionality, it did lay the foundation for future releases by improving performance and reducing the memory footprint.[56] I am not suggesting that you should necessarily spend a year or more refactoring your product, as Apple did. But it can be more effective to make a concentrated effort and invest two to three months in removing spaghetti code and cleaning up the software, as opposed to doing it in drips and drops across several releases. If a refactoring release is the right approach for you, then your roadmap should reflect this and show a release dedicated to making the necessary technical changes.

On People

You may also find that your roadmap is constrained by dependencies on people. The UX expert, for instance, may not be available for a release, or marketing may not have the bandwidth to support it. If you cannot hire more UX experts or marketers, you will have to adjust your product roadmap and change the release contents (or their sequence) to account for these constraints.

---

56 The release became publicly available in August 2009. For more information, see http://en.wikipedia.org/wiki/Mac_OS_X_Snow_Leopard.

If you repeatedly experience that not enough people with the right skills are available, then you should determine the underlying causes. It may be that your company is working on too many products at once or that there are no stable product teams. If that's the case, explore how you could help reduce the number of products being worked on concurrently and how you could create stable cross-functional teams for your product. Doing too much at once and working with changing teams can lead to suboptimal products, poor productivity, and low morale.

But it might also be the case that the people on the development team are highly specialized and therefore cannot help with other design, programming, and test tasks. In this case, I recommend cross-skilling people, for instance, by encouraging the individuals to work in pairs. Bear in mind, though, that cross-skilling people takes time, and there is usually a limit to the number of skills people can acquire and the proficiency they can develop.

On Other Products

Finally, don't forget that your product may have dependencies on other products, which may influence your roadmap. Take the example of one of my clients, a major games studio. The group I have worked with develops physics engines: complex pieces of software that do all the clever animation in computer games. Without them, the characters would make slow, robotic movements, and playing the game would not be fun. A physics engine is not stand-alone product, but is integrated into one or more games. As a consequence, the launch dates and the animation needs of the games influence the product roadmap of the physics engine, and the product manager of the engine has regular meetings with his game-producing counterparts to review, change, and align their roadmaps. A portfolio roadmap can be useful for managing the relationships between different products, as I discuss later, at the end of Part 2.

Be aware that the more dependencies exist, the harder it is to create a realistic roadmap. Ideally, you would like to have your product loosely coupled to the other products your company provides so that you can release new features quickly. If the dependencies feel restrictive, then it may be time to break some of them by changing the products or the teams. To change and realign the products, you may have to unbundle a product and turn a feature into a new product; conversely, you may want to bundle smaller products into a larger one; or you may want to encapsulate shared assets, components, or services in a platform, as described in Part 1. Whatever method you choose, keep in mind that these changes are likely to require a certain level of architecture refactoring, which should be reflected in your product roadmap.

To improve the teams and their setup, form dedicated product teams and ensure that each team works on one product. You should also consider employing feature teams that deliver end-to-end functionality and can implement an entire user story. Feature teams tend to have fewer dependencies than teams that are organized around components, services, and other architecture building blocks; they also allow you to move faster and try out new ideas more quickly. They are thus particularly useful for products that haven't yet entered the maturity stage.

Table 8 summarizes the three different dependency types, together with their recommended actions.

TABLE 8: Roadmap Dependencies

Type	Description	Action
Releases	Dependencies between individual releases on your product roadmap.	Order your releases so that your product progresses effectively from one release to the next. You may choose, for example, to dedicate a release to reworking the user experience or the architecture before adding any major new features.
People	Dependencies on individuals.	Hire or contract more people with the right skills or adjust your roadmap. Work with dedicated cross-functional product teams and consider cross-skilling people.
Products	Dependencies between your product and other products.	Break the dependencies so that the products are loosely coupled, particularly if your product is young or the market is dynamic. For example, unbundle, bundle, or create shared assets or a platform. Adjust or change the team setup. Consider working with feature teams.

Conway's Law

Being affected by product dependencies is very common for digital products in my experience. I have seen e-commerce websites, for instance, where adding a new feature required changes to several other products and systems. Why are there so many product dependencies? Conway's Law offers an explanation.[57] In the late 1960s, the computer scientist Melvin Conway observed that the architecture of your product is likely to mirror your organizational structure. If the organization that is developing the product is complex, then this will be reflected in the software—it is likely to be complex, too, and will probably have many dependencies. To avoid falling prey to Conway's Law, start small; scale up in a controlled, stepwise fashion; and ensure that you have the right team setup.

Make Your Roadmap Measurable

When you go on a road trip and decide to visit a tourist attraction along the way, take a break at a rest stop, or stop overnight at a hotel, you can tell whether the attraction was interesting, the food was good, and the hotel was comfortable. In the same way, you should be able to tell if the releases on your roadmap have the anticipated impact and deliver the desired benefits. This allows you to see if you are executing the product strategy well, and if the strategy is working.

When using a goal-oriented roadmap, ensure that every release goal is *measurable*. For instance, if your goal is to acquire customers, ask yourself how many new customers should be acquired; or if your goal is to reduce technical debt, determine how much of the bad code should be removed or rewritten. If you don't state a target, it will be hard to tell if you have met the goal or not. Make sure, though, that you state a realistic target, and that the goals on your roadmap are realistic. Then select the metrics that will help you determine if a goal has been met and if a release has delivered the desired benefit. For in-

---

57 See https://en.wikipedia.org/wiki/Conway%27s_law.

stance, if your goal is to acquire customers and increase the customer base by 10 percent, then determine *how* you are going to measure if or not the target has been met. For example, does a successful user acquisition require that an individual registers with your website? Does it mean that the person downloads and activates your product? Or should you measure if the number of unique visits has been increased? Similarly, if your goal is to reduce technical debt by half, are you then going to measure if the code complexity or the refactoring potential has been decreased?

In addition, state *by when* the goal should be met. In the case of an acquisition goal, you will probably have to wait a few days or even weeks after the release before enough data will become available to understand whether or not the goal has been met. Finally, make sure that the metrics you use help measure goal attainment. Don't mistake a measurement for an objective. The number of activations is a metric, for example, but the goal is to acquire users. Always choose your goal first; then determine the appropriate metrics. Include the metrics in your roadmap, as I have done in my GO roadmap template; this creates transparency and avoids confusion.

On a feature-based roadmap, state the expected benefit of each release, assuming that you have grouped features into coherent releases. Otherwise, determine the desired benefit each feature should provide, and then follow the recommendations above and select the appropriate metrics.

ROADMAP CHANGES

It can be tempting to view the product roadmap as a hard-and-fast plan that simply needs to be executed well. But the product roadmap is not static. It will change as new ideas appear, new competitors enter the market, the development progress is slower than anticipated, technologies change, or the architecture requires refactoring, for instance. Ignoring these developments is likely to turn the roadmap into an outdated plan that will create unrealistic expectations and provide little benefit. The following practices help you review and update your product roadmap.

Track the Progress

Once you have started building the actual product, track your progress to understand if the release you are working on can be delivered as expected. If it cannot, then you may have to change your product roadmap. A handy tool for recording and anticipating the progress is the *release burndown chart* shown in Figure 45—assuming that you use a Scrum-based process.[58] If you use Kanban, then employ a *cumulative flow diagram* instead.[59] No matter what tool you choose, it should help you understand how you are performing

---

58 The release burndown chart was first described by Schwaber and Beedle (2002).
59 See Cohn (2005) for more information on release burndown charts, and Anderson (2010) for cumulative workflow diagrams.

against the product roadmap, and if the roadmap is valid or needs to be updated.

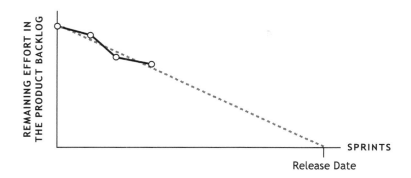

FIGURE 45: Release Burndown Chart

In the sample release burndown chart in Figure 45, the vertical axis captures the remaining effort in the product backlog required to create the next release.[60] On the horizontal axis, the chart states the desired release date, which you may have determined by identifying the window of opportunity (as discussed earlier in the section "Determine the Window of Opportunity"). The first data point on the chart is the estimated effort of the entire product backlog before any development has taken place.[61] To arrive at the next data point, you determine the remaining effort in the product backlog at the end of the first sprint. Then draw a line between the two points. This line is called the *burndown*. The burndown of the third sprint in the chart above is slower than the burndown of the second sprint. This might be caused by a drop in velocity, such as team members being unavailable due to vacation, illness, or training, but it could also be due to product backlog

---

60   I like to work with story points as the estimation unit for product backlog items, but you should apply the measure your team actually uses. For more information on story points, see Cohn (2005).

61   This assumes that the development team is able to provide high-level estimates for all product backlog items that participate in the release.

changes. Based on the data collected from exposing the latest product increment to the customers and users, you might have updated the backlog and added more items to it.

The burndown line shows the progress that has been made, and after a few sprints you should see a trend emerge and be able to forecast future progress. The forecast is represented by the dotted line in the chart above. Luckily, this line predicts that everything is on track, and that the backlog items can be delivered within the desired time frame. But it may well be that the forecast does not look as bright, and all the work cannot be completed on time. If that's the case, then you should investigate the causes. The release goal may be overambitious and unrealistic, the release date may be too aggressive, or the development team may be lacking manpower or skills. To find out why you are off track, get together with the development team and perform a root-cause analysis. Once you have determined the cause, use your primary success factor to take the right action. Weaken the goal, push out the release date, or increase the budget by adding a UX designer or Java specialist to the team, for example. Then update the product roadmap, as I describe in the next section.

Review and Change the Roadmap

As pointed out earlier, the product roadmap is not a fixed plan that is created once and then simply executed. Instead, it needs to be reviewed and adjusted on a regular basis. This section helps you choose the right review frequency, involve the right people, and use the right factors to make the necessary changes.

Review Frequency

How often you should review the product roadmap depends on the maturity of your product and the stability of the market, as Figure 46 shows.

	DYNAMIC MARKET	STABLE MARKET
MATURE PRODUCT	REVIEW QUARTERLY	REVIEW EVERY 3 TO 6 MONTHS
YOUNG PRODUCT	REVIEW MONTHLY	REVIEW QUARTERLY

FIGURE 46: Roadmap Review Matrix

As a rule of thumb, the more uncertainty and change are present, the more frequently you should review your product roadmap. If your product is young and the market is dynamic, for instance, you should review your product roadmap on a monthly basis. If your product is mature but the market keeps changing, or if the market is stable but your product is still young, then I recommend quarterly reviews; and if your product has reached maturity and the market is stable, you can afford to adjust the roadmap every three to six months. When in doubt, use too many rather than too few roadmap reviews: it's better to revisit the roadmap too often than to work with an outdated plan.

If you have to adjust your product roadmap more often than once per month, this may indicate that it is too detailed and carries too many features. As mentioned earlier, I recommend showing no more than five features per release and capturing product capabilities instead of detailed functionality. The latter should be in the product backlog and not in the roadmap.

Stakeholder Involvement
Involve the stakeholders in reviewing and updating the product roadmap. This ensures that the changes are feasible and that people will buy

into the updated roadmap. But don't forget to lead the roadmapping work. As mentioned previously, be careful not to say yes to every idea or request, as this will turn the roadmap into a wish list rather than an actionable plan. Use the product strategy to make the right decisions (assuming it is still valid). Ask the ScrumMaster or coach to facilitate the review so that you can focus on updating the roadmap.

If you use Scrum to develop the product, you can employ the sprint review meeting to reflect on your roadmap. All key stakeholders should be present at this meeting, and you should have the latest development progress and customer and user data available. This saves you from having to set up another meeting, and it connects the strategic planning activities with the tactical ones. If your sprints are two weeks long, for example, then have a bigger sprint review meeting at the end of every second sprint, when you can also take a look at the product roadmap (assuming that a monthly review frequency is appropriate).

Review Factors

When reviewing the product roadmap, take into account any changes in the product strategy, the progress of the work, and the data you have collected from the customers and users, as Figure 47 shows.

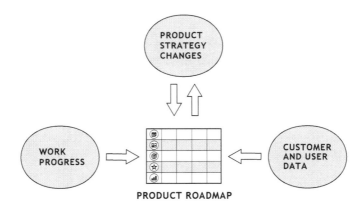

FIGURE 47: Product Roadmap Review Factors

Any changes in the product strategy usually require that you adjust the product roadmap accordingly. This ensures that the roadmap is still an actionable plan that states how the strategy is implemented. Be aware, however, that changes in the product roadmap can also affect the product strategy, as I discuss in more detail below.

The development progress, as captured by a release burndown chart or a cumulative workflow diagram, indicates if you manage to deliver the releases with their goals and features on time and on budget. To be sure that everything is on track, also take into account the progress made by the other stakeholders: Is the marketing and sales work on track, for example? Will the relevant deliverables, such as the marketing and sales collateral, be available as planned? And if not, what effect will this have on the roadmap?

The data collected from the customers and users helps you understand if the goals and features on the product roadmap are correct, and if you are providing the right user experience and features in the right way. Collect the data by exposing product increments to the customers and users—for instance, by employing a product demo, running a usability test, or releasing the software. This is particularly helpful when your product is young or when you are revitalizing an aging product. Adjust the goals and features according to the insights you've gained from analyzing the data.

Incremental Changes vs. Pivots

Based on the progress and the customer and user data, you may need to refine the product roadmap by, for example, adjusting a goal or replacing a feature. But such an incremental change may not be enough. Take the case of Instagram, which started as a location-aware service and then changed to a picture- and video-sharing product. And Instagram is not alone: Flickr was once an online role-playing game, and YouTube was a video-dating site (Love 2011). As these examples show, strategy changes or pivots can occur after the launch of a product—whether users employ the product in unanticipated ways, as in the case of Flickr, or a competitor significantly changes the market. You should consequently be open to big, radical roadmap changes, particularly when you are managing a new or young product. Whenever you find that your product roadmap does not work, analyze the causes and investigate if the product strategy is still valid. Don't massage the roadmap when deeper changes are required—this would be like buying a better map or choosing a new route when traveling by car will not get you to your destination.

PORTFOLIO ROADMAPS

All for one and one for all.
Alexandre Dumas

This chapter provides a brief overview of portfolio roadmaps. While I can't cover the topic in more detail in this book, the good news is that you can apply most of the concepts and techniques discussed in the previous chapters to your portfolio roadmap.

Why You Should Use a Portfolio Roadmap

Products don't exist in isolation. Instead, they are often related to other products that they help sell or share features and components with. Think of the Microsoft Office suite or the iPod product line. If your product is part of a portfolio, you will benefit from a portfolio roadmap: a plan that shows how the products are likely to grow together. This makes it easier to coordinate the development and launch of the products, and it helps you identify and manage dependencies between them. If your product is constrained by a large number of dependencies, however, then a portfolio roadmap may not be enough; you should also address the dependencies, as I described in the section "Take Dependencies into Account."

Plan Your Portfolio with the GO Portfolio Roadmap

Let's explore how you can capture your portfolio roadmap. Figure 48 shows my preferred version of a portfolio roadmap, which is based on the GO roadmap format introduced earlier in this part.

DATE/TIME FRAME					
PORTFOLIO a	**PRODUCT A**				
	Goal				
	Features				
	Metrics				
	PRODUCT B				
	Goal				
	Features				
	Metrics				

FIGURE 48: The GO Portfolio Roadmap

The GO portfolio roadmap in Figure 48 is a goal-oriented roadmap that combines the roadmaps of several related products into a single plan. Its top section displays the release dates or time frames. It then states the portfolio with its products: product A and product B. Each product has its own goals, features, and metrics that are identical to their counterpart in the GO product roadmap. Each goal describes the desired benefit a major release should provide, the features that make up the key deliverables necessary to meet the goal, and the metrics will be used to determine if the goal has been met. You can add more products to a portfolio, of course, and you can also extend the structure shown in Figure 48 by adding one or more portfolios. If the GO portfolio roadmap resonates with you, then you can download it from my website, where more information on this tool is available.

Let's see how the GO portfolio roadmap can be applied by building on the healthy-eating app example used previously.

DATE/TIME FRAME		Q1	Q2	Q3
HEALTHY-EATING PORTFOLIO	BEACH BODY APP	V4	V5	V6
	Goal	Future-proofing	Revenue	Retention
	Features	Architecture refactoring	In-app purchases: recipes, exercise videos	UX updates; enhanced calorie counter
	Metrics	Code complexity reduced by 30%	Revenue increased by 5-10%	Engagement increased by 10-15%
	TRAINING APP	V1	V2	V3
	Goal	Acquisition: cyclists and runners	Retention	Revenue
	Features	Calorie counter, dashboard, activity tracker	Nutrition advice, enhanced dashboard	Virtual dietitian
	Metrics	1,000 new users	Engagement increased by 5-10%	5% of users make in-app purchase

FIGURE 49: Sample GO Portfolio Roadmap

The sample portfolio roadmap in Figure 49 consists of one portfolio, the Healthy Eating product family, and two fictitious products, the Beach Body app and the Training app. The former is aimed at people who would like to lose weight to look slimmer; the latter targets athletes who would like to improve their performance by adjusting their diet. As Figure 49 shows, major releases are planned for both products on a quarterly basis. While the Beach Body app has been available for a while, the Training app is currently in development. If the latter reuses features of the former, but those features first have to be refactored, then the roadmap in Figure 49 contains dependencies. These dependencies have to be managed, and the roadmap may have to be reworked by, for instance, delaying the launch of the training app to Q2. This illustrates one of the main benefits of a portfolio roadmap: it is easier to spot dependencies compared with using separate product roadmaps. If I decided to bundle the components shared by the two products in a separate platform, I would add the platform to the portfolio. This would allow me to coordinate the development of the platform and the two apps.

Address These Portfolio Challenges

While using portfolio roadmaps can be very beneficial, it introduces an additional level of interaction compared with using individual product roadmaps. The product manager of the Beach Body app, for instance, has to coordinate with the product manager of the Training app to create the portfolio roadmap in Figure 49. If the portfolio is larger, then it may be beneficial to have a dedicated portfolio manager. The individual leads the effort of creating and changing the portfolio roadmap, helps resolve dependencies between products, sets priorities across products, and makes decisions when the product managers cannot agree. Figure 50 shows the new role, together with other portfolio roadmap beneficiaries.

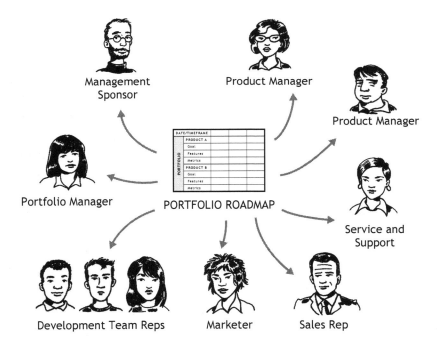

FIGURE 50: Portfolio Roadmap and Stakeholders

Because developing and updating a portfolio roadmap tends to be more challenging compared with a product roadmap—not least because more people are involved—I recommend that you develop a solid *product* roadmapping practice before you employ portfolio roadmaps.

EPILOGUE

In theory, there is no difference between theory and practice.
But in practice, there is.
Yogi Berra[62]

"I don't think we should use product roadmaps. They are inflexible and anti-agile," said the head of sales in a workshop I ran a few years ago for a client. We were discussing how to improve the company's product management capabilities, and I had suggested that the product managers should employ product roadmaps to capture strategic product decisions. Initially, the response took me by surprise, and I thought that the company might have been applying product roadmaps incorrectly. But further discussion revealed the true reason: the executives were making all the strategic decisions. The product managers were expected to implement them, write user stories, and manage the product backlogs. They were not properly empowered, and they lacked the authority and skills to shape the strategy of their products.

It would be nice to think of this story as a one-off. But experience tells me that's not the case: many other companies face similar challenges. Their root cause is the lack of an effective product management function—a dedicated group of product people who are respected and authorized, who have the trust and the support of the executive man-

---

62 This quote is also attributed to other individuals including the computer scientist Jan L. A. van de Snepscheut.

agement team, and who are qualified and have the necessary skills to make the right strategic product decisions. Without such a function, leveraging the practices discussed in the book will be difficult.

While the organizational context is undoubtedly important, it would be too easy—and often unrealistic—to expect that executive management provides the perfect product management environment. As the individual in charge of a product, you have to ask what *you* can do to ensure that the right strategic decisions are made. This often requires the willingness to lead, guide, and influence others, to be proactive, and to show initiative; it might even include making a decision rather than waiting for an official authorization—if the latter would endanger the success of the product.

Finally, to take advantage of the concepts, techniques, and tools described in this book, you have to put them into practice. Don't be disheartened when this isn't straightforward. Learning takes time, and making strategic decisions can be tough. As the Lao Tzu quote at the beginning of the book says, "A journey of a thousand miles begins with a single step." Take the first step now, and try some of the techniques discussed in this book. I wish you all the best for your journey.

ABOUT THE AUTHOR

Roman Pichler works as a product management consultant, teacher, and writer. He has a long track record of training and mentoring product managers and helping companies improve their product management capabilities. He is the author of the book *Agile Product Management with Scrum* and he writes a popular product management blog. As the founder and director of Pichler Consulting, Roman looks after the company's products and services. This keeps his product management practice fresh, and it allows him to experiment with new ideas. Roman lives with his wife and three children near London, United Kingdom. You can contact Roman at info@romanpichler.com, and you can find out more about his work at www.romanpichler.com.

REFERENCES

Anderson, D. 2010. *Kanban.* Blue Hole Press.

Ansoff, I. 1957. "Strategies for Diversification." *Harvard Business Review* 35 (5): 113–24.

Baker, M., and S. Hart. 2007. *Product Strategy and Management.* 2nd Ed. Financial Times/Prentice Hall.

Blank, S. 2014. "The Key to Startup Success: Get out of the Building." *Inc. Video The Playbook*, November 2. Accessed November 23, 2015. http://www.inc.com/steve-blank/key-to-success-getting-out-of-building.html.

Brown, T. 2009. *Change by Design.* HarperBusiness.

Cagan, M. 2011. "Reviewing the Product Discovery Team and Its Roles." May 8. Accessed November 23, 2015. https://www.youtube.com/watch?v=734K7cEo30U.

Christensen, C. M. 1997. *The Innovator's Dilemma: When New Technologies Cause Great Firms to Fail.* Harvard Business School Press.

Christensen, C. M., and M. E. Raynor. 2013. *The Innovator's Solution, Revised and Expanded: Creating and Sustaining Successful Growth.* 2nd Ed. Harvard Business Review Press.

Cohn, M. 2005. *Agile Estimating and Planning.* Prentice Hall.

Constine, J. 2015. "Facebook Launches Messenger Platform for Content Tools and Chat with Businesses." *TechCrunch*, March 25. Accessed November 23, 2015. http://techcrunch.com/2015/03/25/facebook-launches-messenger-platform-with-content-tools-and-chat-with-businesses/#.ldrked:YRev.

Cooper, A. 1999. *The Inmates Are Running the Asylum.* Sams Publishing.

Coyne, K. 2008. "Enduring Ideas: The GE–McKinsey nine-box matrix." McKinsey Quarterly, September. Accessed February 10, 2016. http://www.mckinsey.com/insights/strategy/enduring_ideas_the_ge_and_mckinsey_nine-box_matrix

Croll, A., and B. Yoskovitz. 2013. *Lean Analytics. Use Data to Build a Better Startup Faster.* O'Reilly Media.

D'Orazio, D. 2014. "Google Splits Up Drive App, Requires Standalone Apps to Edit Documents." *The Verge*, May 3. Accessed November 23, 2015. http://www.theverge.com/2014/5/3/5678494/google-drive-updated-removes-document-editing.

Downes, L., and P. Nunes. 2013. "Big-Bang Disruption." *Harvard Business Review* (May): 44–56.

Drucker, P. F. 1985. *Innovation and Entrepreneurship.* Harper & Row.

Eden, C., and F. Ackermann. 2011. *Making Strategy: Mapping Out Strategic Success.* 2nd Ed. SAGE Publications.

Elizalde, D. 2014. "3 Ways Gran Turismo Takes Product Management to the Next Level." Techproductmanagement.com, November 13. Accessed November 23, 2015. http://techproductmanagement.com/3-ways-gran-turismo-takes-product-management-to-the-next-level/.

Fisher, D. 2008. "How Google Developed the Chrome Web Browser." (C. Frye, Interviewer). SearchSoftwareQuality.com, October 1. Accessed February 10, 2016. http://searchsoftwarequality.techtarget.com/news/1332788/How-Google-developed-the-Chrome-Web-browser

Howard, J. 2013. "5 Amazing Examples of Successful Rebranding." *Pencil Scoop*, April 12. Accessed November 23, 2015. http://pencilscoop.com/2013/04/5-amazing-examples-of-successful-rebranding.

Islam, N., and S. Ozcan. 2012. "Disruptive Product Innovation Strategy: The Case of Portable Digital Music Players." In *Disruptive Technologies, Innovation and Global Redesign: Emerging Implications.* By N. Ekekwe, edited by N. Ekekwe and I. Nazrul, 27–45. IGI Global.

Jobs, S. 2015. "iPhone Keynote 2007." *Genius*, March. Accessed November 23, 2015. http://genius.com/Steve-jobs-iPhone-keynote-2007-annotated.

Jones, J. P., and D. Womack. 2005. *Lean Solutions. How Companies and Customers Can Create Value Together.* Simon & Schuster.

Kano, N. 1984. "Attractive Quality and Must-Be Quality." *Journal of the Japanese Society for Quality Control* (April): 39–48.

Kerzner, H. R. 2013. *Project Management: A Systems Approach to Planning, Scheduling, and Controlling.* 11th Ed. John Wiley & Sons.

Kim, W. C., and R. Mauborgne. 2004. *Blue Ocean Strategy.* Harvard Business Review Press.

Kouzes, J., and P. Barry. 2012. *The Leadership Challenge: How to Make Extraordinary Things Happen in Organizations.* 5th Ed. John Wiley & Sons.

Lapowsky, I. 2013. "Ev Williams on Twitter's Early Years." *Inc.com*, October 4. Accessed November 23, 2015. www.inc.com/issie-lapowsky/ev-williams-twitter-early-years.html.

Levitt, T. 1965. "Exploit the Product Life Cycle." *Harvard Business Review* 43: 81–94.

Liker, J. 2004. *The Toyota Way: 14 Management Principles from the World's Greatest Manufacturer.* McGraw-Hill Professional.

Love, D. 2011. "The 15 Greatest Tech Pivots Ever." *Business Insider*, May 3. Accessed November 2015. www.businessinsider.com/most-successful-pivots-2011-4.

Maurya, A. 2012. *Running Lean. Iterate from Plan A to a Plan That Works.* 2nd Ed. O'Reilly Media.

Moon, Y. 2005. "Break Free from the Product Life Cycle." *Harvard Business Review* (May): 86–94.

Moore, G. 2006. *Crossing the Chasm. Marketing and Selling Disruptive Products to Mainstream Customers.* Collins Business Essentials.

Nagji, B., and G. Tuff. 2012. "Managing Your Innovation Portfolio." *Harvard Business Review* (May): 66–74.

Norton, D. P., and R. S. Kaplan. 1996. *The Balanced Scorecard: Translating Strategy into Action.* Harvard Business School Press.

Osterwalder, A., and Y. Pigneur. 2010. *Business Model Generation.* John Wiley & Sons.

Pichler, R. 2010. *Agile Product Management with Scrum: Creating Products that Customers Love.* Addison-Wesley.

Preece, C. 2015. "iPad Mini Sales Hit by iPhone 6 Plus Popularity." *IT-PRO*, January 7. Accessed November 23, 2015. http://www.itpro.co.uk/tablets/23799/ipad-mini-sales-hit-by-iPhone-6-plus-popularity.

Ries, A., and J. Trout. 1994. *The 22 Immutable Laws of Marketing*. Profile Books.

Ries, E. 2009. "Built to Learn." *Startup Lessons Learned*, April 9. Accessed January 5, 2016. http://www.startuplessonslearned.com/2009/04/built-to-learn.html.

———. 2009. "Vanity Metrics vs. Actionable Metrics." *The Tim Ferriss Experiment*, May 19. Accessed November 23, 2015. http://fourhourworkweek.com/2009/05/19/vanity-metrics-vs-actionable-metrics/.

———. 2009. "Minimum Viable Product." Slideshare, July 22. http://www.slideshare.net/startuplessonslearned/minimum-viable-product.

———. 2011. *The Lean Startup: How Constant Innovation Creates Radically Successful Businesses*. Portfolio Penguin.

Schwaber, K., and M. Beedle. 2002. *Agile Software Development with SCRUM*. Prentice Hall.

Smith, P., and R. Pichler. 2005. "Agile Risks, Agile Rewards." *Software Development Magazine*, April, 50–53.

Tuckman, B. 1965. "Developmental Sequence in Small Groups." *Psychological Bulletin* 63: 384–99.

Wysocki, R. K. 2013. *Effective Project Management: Traditional, Agile, Extreme*. 7th Ed. Wiley.

INDEX

Made in the USA
Lexington, KY
15 September 2017